THE PARABLE AND ITS LESSON

STANFORD STUDIES IN JEWISH HISTORY AND CULTURE

EDITED BY Aron Rodrigue and Steven J. Zipperstein

THE PARABLE AND ITS LESSON

a novella

S.Y. AGNON

TRANSLATED AND ANNOTATED BY
JAMES S. DIAMOND

WITH AN INTRODUCTION AND CRITICAL ESSAY BY
ALAN MINTZ

STANFORD UNIVERSITY PRESS
STANFORD, CALIFORNIA

Stanford University Press
Stanford, California

The Parable and Its Lesson was originally published in Hebrew in 1973 under the
title *Hamashal vehanimshal*, having appeared as one of several stories in the volume
'Ir umelo'ah © 1973, Schocken. The English translation is printed with permission.

Printed in the United States of America on acid-free, archival-quality paper

Library of Congress Cataloging-in-Publication Data

Agnon, Shmuel Yosef, 1888-1970, author.
 [Mashal veha-nimshal. English]
 The parable and its lesson : a novella / S.Y. Agnon ; translated and annotated by
James S. Diamond ; with an introduction and critical essay by Alan Mintz.
      pages cm--(Stanford studies in Jewish history and culture)
 "Originally published in Hebrew in 1973 under the title Hamashal vehanimshal, having
appeared as one of several stories in the volume 'Ir umelo'ah."
 ISBN 978-0-8047-8871-1 (cloth : alk. paper)--
 ISBN 978-0-8047-8872-4 (pbk. : alk. paper)
 1. Jews--Ukraine--Buchach--Fiction. I. Diamond, James S., translator. II. Mintz,
Alan L., writer of introduction, writer of added commentary. III. Title. IV. Series:
Stanford studies in Jewish history and culture.
 PJ5053.A4M3513 2014
 892.43'5--dc23   2013039418
 ISBN 978-0-8047-8925-7 (electronic)

Designed by Bruce Lundquist
Typeset at Stanford University Press in 11/15 Adobe Garamond

James S. Diamond (1939–2013)
IN MEMORIAM

CONTENTS

Printed with permission of Beit Agnon.

INTRODUCTION

ALAN MINTZ

The decisions of the Nobel committee on literature have often been curious, but the award of the prize for 1966 to S. Y. Agnon (together with Nelly Sachs) was not one of those instances. At the time, Agnon was generally regarded as the greatest modern Hebrew writer, and the prize richly deserved. It was also an important moment for Israel and its citizens because this was the first time—and so far the only time—a Hebrew writer was given the award, and the honor was taken as a recognition of the achievements of this new literature in general. Agnon lived just long enough to take great pleasure in the honor and to enjoy the tributes given him not only in Israel but in the United States, which he visited for the first time the year after the award. Agnon died in 1970 at the age of eighty-two.

Agnon's output was prodigious. He wrote and published continuously from 1905 to his death, after which fourteen more volumes appeared, to be placed alongside the several versions of the collected stories and novels that came out in his lifetime. Agnon was a ceaseless rewriter, and there is scarcely a major text in his oeuvre that has not undergone several revisions. Although Agnon's forte was the story in all its short and long forms, he also wrote five major novels and devoted himself to compiling thematic anthologies of Jewish classical sources. Rather than turning from one form and immersing himself in another, Agnon would typically work on several projects in different genres at one time. Because the ongoing body of his work is dynamic, polyphonic and unstable, it has been difficult for critics to divide Agnon's career into usefully identifiable phases. Yet despite these challenges, most students of Agnon would point to the twenty years following his return to Palestine from Germany in 1924 as the high water mark in the master's career. All of his novels were published or written during this time, as were the modernist parables collected in *The Book of Deeds* [Sefer Hama'asim]. These latter were the stories that changed the way contemporary readers perceived Agnon. Initially viewing him as a teller of naïve tales of Polish Jewry, readers subsequently came to accept him as an ironic modern master.

From the end of World War Two to his death, Agnon continued to write, revise and publish prolifically, but the work produced during this period seemed to most critics to be a continuation of the various modes, genres and themes of his earlier writing. It is generally assumed that this creative activity was aimed at tying up loose ends, bringing projects to fruition and extending the range of previously secured innovations.

It is now clear that this conception of Agnon's last phase needs to undergo a fundamental revision. We can now see that one of Agnon's postwar projects was entirely new: a preoccupying, ambitious, large-scale undertaking that represented a fundamental rethinking of the master's relationship to the world of Eastern Europe. This is the epic cycle of stories—close to 150 of them—written during the 1950s and 1960s about Buczacz, the Galician town, today in the eastern Ukraine, in which Agnon grew up and lived until his emigration to Palestine at the age of nineteen in 1907. None of the material appears in any earlier collection. The whole was compiled by the Agnon's daughter Emumah Yaron, according to her father's instructions, and published under the title *'Ir umelo'ah* [*A City in Its Fullness*] in 1973. The story cycle endeavors to give an account of Buczacz during the two hundred years that followed the devastating Khmelnitski massacres of 1648. Taken together, the stories constitute Agnon's comprehensive effort, after the annihilation of

European Jewry, to think through the question of what from that lost culture should be retrieved through the resources of the literary imagination. *'Ir umelo'ah* was hardly noticed when it was published, and it remains largely unknown to the non-Hebrew reading world. Yet I would argue that it is one of the most extraordinary responses to the murder of European Jewry in modern Jewish writing. *Hamashal vehanimshal*, the novella from that collection presented and translated here as *The Parable and Its Lesson*, reaches back in time to explore the responses to the 1648 massacres in light of our implicit awareness of the great catastrophe of our era. It is a good representative of the larger project of the Buczacz tales because it is concerned both with capturing the pathos of a historical moment in the fortunes of the city and with the ways in which narrative and voice refract reality. Agnon's passion remained the disingenuous act of storytelling. *The Parable and Its Lesson*, with its two narrators and sustained monologue and intriguing fissures, provides an excellent instance of Agnon's mature narrative energies at full tilt.

What is Agnon for us today? Does he number among those once-famous writers who now seem to belong to another time and another world of taste? To be sure, his portrait and quotations from his Nobel Prize speech appear on the fifty-shekel note in Israel, but that only guarantees him a place alongside other forgotten founders. Or does Agnon's work qualify as being a true classic, if we understand a classic as literature that, despite its rootedness in a particular time and place and conventions of writing, nonetheless possesses enough surplus of meaning to speak to us now? For the present, Agnon's place among cultured readers in Israel is secure, although the increasing polarization between secular and religious culture may eventually endanger that status; for the former he may come to seem too foreign and the for latter impure simply for being literature. For young people, Agnon is one of those standard authors you have to get through for exams, even though sensitive readers will often rediscover him as adults. Reading Agnon is not easy. Even committed and discriminating readers who are native speakers of Hebrew have to deal with many unfamiliar references, especially if they lack a background in traditional

Jewish texts. The fact that Agnon continues to be read despite these obstacles provides evidence for the claim that he is indeed a classic.

But for a true classic, there is an additional high hurdle: translatability. When the nuances and the echoes and puns and the rhythm are shorn from the work, does it still excite us? In Agnon's case the record is mixed. The translators who have sought to preserve the special strangeness of Agnon's Hebrew have been less successful than those who have been willing to sacrifice a great deal in order to create a simulacrum that works as literature in English. It of course makes a great deal of difference what kind of Agnon is being translated. He wrote continuously for more than sixty years, and he wrote in different genres. For example, his first novel, *Hakhnasat kalah* [The Bridal Canopy, 1931] concerns the peregrinations of a poor Hasid in search of a dowry for his daughters among the townlets of Galicia in the early nineteenth century. This sprawling comic narrative is heavy with biblical allusions and parodies of religious practices and anecdotes about rabbinic sages. Putting such a work into English—it was done, unevenly, by I. M. Lask in 1967—throws up a very different set of problems than works written in a mode closer to European realism, such as Agnon's second novel, *Sipur pashut* [A Simple Story, 1935], translated, superbly, by Hillel Halkin in 1985. Set in Agnon's hometown of Buczacz in the years before World War One, the novel follows the psychological breakdown and recovery of the son of an established merchant family. Although here too there are allusions and submerged subtexts, the object of representation is a much more familiar bourgeois world in which religious learning plays little role.

For the present occasion, we have gone to the difficult end of the Agnon spectrum and chosen to translate a work that poses steep challenges and, because it is a riveting work of art, offers steep rewards as well. First published in *Haaretz* in 1958, *The Parable and Its Lesson* is not well known even to aficionados of Agnon in Israel. Set in the late seventeenth century, it is an account of the journey taken by a rabbi and his shamash, his assistant, into Gehinnom, the Underworld, for the purpose of freeing a teenage bride from the bonds of widowhood. The scenes of horrible and peculiar torments they witness there are gruesome in themselves; worse still are the received notions of sin and punishment that they seem to overturn. The journey to Gehinnom is described as part of the testimony that the shamash gives in his own defense at a trial that takes place fifty-four years after the events. The story shows us Buczacz at two removes: in the immediate aftermath of the Khmelnitski massacres, the community struggles to reconstitute itself and mourn its losses, and then a half-century later when the now-prosperous community is on the verge of a disturbing complacency.

This is a truly exciting piece of literature that is unparalleled in the rest of modern Jewish writing. It is also difficult, difficult in Hebrew, and in translation all the more so. This difficulty comes in several specific varieties, and it has been our aim in this edition to account for them and compensate for them in various ways. First, we have provided a glossary of Hebrew terms for readers who are not familiar with traditional Jewish life. We have retained a number of Hebrew terms in the translation—and naturalized them by not italicizing them—because there are simply no adequate English equivalents. A chief example is the main character of the story. To call the shamash, the assistant who accompanies the rabbi on the journey to Gehinnom, a sexton or a beadle is awkward and foreign to the historical context.

Second, we have provided an extensive set of notes that explain biblical allusions, references to the rabbinic literature and medieval compositions, theological concepts from Kabbalah, abstruse ritual practices and relevant historical events. We have chosen not to interfere with the flow of the text by placing endnote or footnote numbers next to the terms that are explained in the notes; rather, we have placed the notes at the end and marked them according to the pages on which appear the terms they explain. They are there, in other words, for those who want them. There are different kinds of readers. For some, the story can be read with pleasure and understanding without recourse to much of the information in the notes; and this is not because that information is already known but because it is not truly necessary to take in the story. Other readers feel intrigued or provoked by unfamiliar references, and they wish to have that gap filled in even if it means an interruption in the flow of reading.

Finally, there are difficulties that have little to do with translation or cultural literacy. These are perplexing interpretive problems that are inherent in the story. Why does the shamash wait a half century to tell his story? What practical purpose is served by the rabbi's descent into Gehinnom? Why does the story devote so much attention to the ceremonies commemorating the dead of 1648? Why did Agnon name the story *The Parable and Its Lesson* when the parable in question contributes little to our enlightenment? Hence the usefulness of the interpretative essay that accompanies the story. The essay first describes how Agnon embarked on the massive cycle of the Buczacz stories as a unique response to the murder of European Jewry and how he developed a set of narrative techniques for this project that required a departure from how he wrote in the past. The essay then enters the thicket of interpretive difficulties in the story itself and proposes ways of reading that attempt to make sense of Agnon's narrative choices. In sum, it is our wager that even a difficult Agnon text—so long as it is a superb Agnon text, as we believe this one to be—can be enjoyed in translation provided the necessary interpretive resources. We hope that reading this one Buczacz tale will stimulate interest in the larger project of which it is a part.

ACKNOWLEDGMENTS

Ariel Hirschfeld and Jeffrey Saks were always available for us to draw on their erudition and good judgment. I am grateful to David Stern and Raymond Scheindlin for their encouragement and their help in solving knotty problems.

James S. Diamond was killed in a traffic accident shortly after the manuscript of this book was submitted. His death is a grave loss, and he will be greatly missed.

THE PARABLE AND ITS LESSON

S. Y. AGNON
TRANSLATED AND ANNOTATED
BY JAMES S. DIAMOND

AMONG THE LINE OF RABBIS who ruled in our town was the illustrious and godly Rabbi Moshe, a rabbi who, in his lifetime, journeyed to Gehinnom in order to free an agunah. Two purposes motivate me to record this story. One is to tell of the greatness of that saintly rabbi. The other, as I have already noted, is to admonish those among us, old and young alike, who permit themselves to talk during the prayer service and the Torah reading. In Buczacz no one talks during the service and the reading of the Torah. That is the long-standing local custom. But every city has someone who hails from somewhere else, and so it happened that there was in Buczacz just such a man who was unaware of the local custom and chatted while the Torah was being read. This story is about him. It is a story from which we will come to learn what the punishment is for those who conduct conversations during the prayers and the Torah reading. To be sure, some things related here will not square with those who maintain that Buczacz was unaffected by the Khmelnitski pogroms. I leave it to the One who reconciles all matters to settle this one too.

1

There was in our old beit midrash an elderly shamash named Reb Yeruham ben Tanhum. Some insist that his name was Reb Tanhum ben Yeruham and that the Great Synagogue was where he served. Then there are those who claim that this name belongs not to the shamash but to the man who got involved with the him. I, who know only the names of the men who served as shamash in the ten generations before I left my hometown, cannot make this determination. I can only tell the story. Besides, the name itself is immaterial to what follows, even though it is known that a person's essence, not to mention the incarnations through which his soul passes, can be discerned in his name. Let me, then, put aside what I cannot explain and relate what I do know.

A wealthy man from the upper crust of our town took as his son-in-law a learned young man from a prominent family. The boy was skilled at advancing all kinds of novel interpretations of our holy texts, even when their meanings were already transparent. In fact, sometimes, in his encounter with a text, he would pronounce his own interpretation before he had even digested its plain sense. I refer here not to the nature of his insights but to the fact that his eagerness to propose them overrode any capacity he had for self-restraint. That is the gist of this tale, and the details now follow.

One Sabbath, while the Torah was being read, he was sitting in his regular seat against the eastern wall of the synagogue, a prestigious place that his father-in-law bought for him from an old man who had emigrated to the Land of Israel. A Bible with commentaries was in his hands. The reader was chanting from the scroll and the entire congregation was sitting in rapt attention listening to the words of the Torah, when the young man had a brilliant new hidush on that week's Torah portion or on one of its commentaries. He raised his talit over his eyes, leaned over to the man sitting next to him, and shared his hidush with him. The latter looked at him dumbfounded, stunned that someone dared to talk during the Torah reading. As if the words of a mere mortal were superior to those of the living God.

Do not wonder at that man's astonishment, because in our town there was absolutely no talking during the service and certainly not during the Torah reading. From the moment the Torah scroll was opened until the reading of the weekly portion was concluded everyone strained to listen and concentrated so as to catch every word that issued from God Himself. The elders of that time, going by what they had heard from their fathers, and their fathers from their fathers, said that their forebears would never interrupt the Torah reading even to congratulate the person who had just been called up to the Torah. Three times a year, however, on Passover, Shavuot, and Sukkot, after the Yizkor memorial service, the senior member of the congregation would take the Torah scroll in his arms and one by one everyone would come up and tell him his name, his father's name, and the amount he would contribute. The elder would bless that person and his household and there would be no mention of money. Contributions were brought after the festival. In later times, when expenses increased, they started doing this on every Sabbath, but again, money was never mentioned in the presence of the Torah scroll. Then later, when the number of donors who wanted their charitable intentions made public increased, every penny that had been pledged or contributed would be announced. And then even later, when expenses for nonessential items increased, like the fees for cantors who showed off their vocal talents and turned the prayers into ridiculous performances, all prior restraints were removed, and they would stop between sections of the Torah reading to bless both the one who was called up and the person he instructed the gabbai to bless. Soon they began to exceed the regular number of seven people called up to the Torah, until the Torah readings were sliced up like olives. Eventually things reached the point where there was not only jealousy and enmity among the honorees but insult and invective.

So there sits our young scholar during the Torah reading when he gets this new insight into the Torah portion. He leans over to the man sitting next to him and regales him with his discovery. The shamash sees this and throws him a look of rebuke. When this is ignored the shamash gives him a wrathful look. When the talking does not stop he thumps his middle finger with a "Nu! Nu!" When this has no effect the shamash thumps his finger again in order to silence him. When this has no effect he steps down from the bimah, walks over to the eastern wall, grabs the young man by the arm and ushers him out of the synagogue.

The town was in an uproar. Never in the whole history of Buczacz had anyone embarrassed another person in such a holy place, much less ejected him from it. Certainly no lowly shamash had ever done that to a Torah scholar, especially one from a prestigious family and the son-in-law of a local grandee to boot. And even though everyone knew that the shamash had acted for the sake of Heaven, the consensus was to fine him and even to dismiss him from his position.

On Monday they arraigned him before the beit din of the chief rabbi. The chief rabbi recused himself on account of his admitted partiality to Torah scholars. Thereupon they went and constituted an alternate beit din.

The dayan asked the shamash how he proposed to argue his case. The latter replied, "Is anything more meritorious than not kowtowing to a Torah scholar from a prominent family who commingles the Sacred Word with his own prattle?"

The dayan then asked, "But was he not talking words of Torah?"

"Yes, but it was during the reading of the Torah."

"It was sufficient that you stopped him. What impelled you to embarrass him in public?"

"It was out of compassion for him that I did what I did, for I have seen the punishment that awaits one for talking during prayers and Torah reading. A thousand humiliations in this world are nothing compared to the punishment for this transgression in the world to come."

"How is it that you knew and others did not? We have many treatises that deal with that particular sin, and it is widely condemned by our rabbis. Indeed, there are those who attribute the pogroms of 1648 to the sin of talking during the service."

"The books may offer their condemnations, but it is the eyes that see what it is to suffer God's wrath."

"What do you mean 'it is the eyes that see'? Does the whole world see with a different organ and you alone see with eyes? What do you mean by these alarming insinuations?"

The shamash lowered his eyes and fell silent.

The dayan continued, "What do you answer?" The shamash raised his eyes and then shut them, like one who sees something and is mortified by it. What was it that made him so afraid? It was visions that he had once seen, visions that were now reawakened within him and began to reappear before him. It is those visions I shall presently relate.

The dayan looked at him and saw all manner of horror etched in his face. Something is going on, he thought to himself. "Perhaps you can explain to us what you have said?" The shamash again lowered his eyes and said, "One thing I ask of the Lord, one thing I desire: that my mouth not get the better of me and make me utter something that I should not. Would that this whole incident had not happened and I were not forced to relate something of which I am not worthy to speak. Silence would be the better course." He fell silent. The dayan said, "I think there is something you wish to say?" Consternation took hold of the shamash. He raised his eyes to those who sat in judgment of him and began to speak: "It is not because I seek acquittal from this earthly court or because I want to curry favor with the esteemed members of the congregation that I permit my tongue to reveal a profound mystery. I speak so that you may all come to know the true punishment for something that everyone takes much too lightly."

2

The shamash looked out at those who sat in judgment of him and at those who had come to hear his case, and this is what he related:

The venerable elders here are already aware that I served as personal assistant to our Master, the esteemed Av Beit Din Rabbi Moshe, may the Lord illumine him in Eden until the coming of the Redeemer and may he plead well for us and all Israel. I am not worthy to tell of his greatness and his brilliance in Torah and piety. What I can relate is what is widely known, namely, that our Master Rabbi Moshe was, as you know, one of the students of the holy Rabbi Mikhl of Nemirov. On account of our many sins Rabbi Mikhel Mikhl was martyred in the massacres of 1648. Through the merits of one secret word in the Torah that that holy Tsadik communicated to our Master Rabbi Moshe, he was saved from the sword of that barbarian Khmelnitski, may his name be blotted out. Some say the word is in the weekly Torah portion *Mishpatim*. Some say it is in the portion of *Ha'azinu*. Others hold that it was not a word that he communicated but the meaning of one of the dots found above the Hebrew words in the passage *haniglot vehanistarot*. Who can say what that dot means? It is enough for a man like me to get through the weekly portion with Targum and Rashi's commentary.

Our Master had a relative named Zlateh. She was the sole survivor when her family was slaughtered in the pogroms of the abominable Khmelnitski, may the names of the wicked rot. This Zlateh was a granddaughter of Reb Naftali the wine merchant. He was a wonderful advocate for the Jews in his time and did much for communities and individuals alike. He met a tragic end. A government official who owed him four hundred barrels of wine set his hunting dogs on him and they devoured him. May God avenge his blood.

The murder of Reb Naftali occurred not long before the pogroms of 1648. When the evil decree fell, the whole family perished, "some by water, some by fire, some by strangling, some by stoning," as the poet wrote in the piyyut *Unetanneh tokef.* Those who were spared such gruesome deaths died of hunger or thirst. Through the mercy of God the little girl saved herself from death by hiding in the forest. Like an innocent lamb she lived on grass and very nearly forgot how to talk like a human being. She was found by some survivors who had come out of hiding when the pogroms began to abate. They took her with them as they wandered from town to town and from community to community. Some of them tried to return to their hometowns but could not find them. Most of the communities had been razed in the cataclysm and were unrecognizable. Some of these survivors got used to being on the road and never found a place to stop and settle down. During their wanderings they came to Buczacz and arrived at the house of our Master.

The Rabbi's wife looked at the little girl but had no idea who she was. The good qualities that she noticed in her endeared the child to her. She took her in and fed her, clothed her, put shoes on her bare feet. The Rabbi's wife made an arrangement with the people who had brought the girl with them, paying them off so they would leave the child with her. And so they did. The Rabbi's wife asked the girl about her hometown and where she came from and about her father and her mother. The child told what she remembered.

The Rabbi's wife listened to all this and related it to our Master. Upon hearing it he declared, "Is she not of our family? Why, she is a descendant of our relative Naftali!" Our Master raised his sacred hands and intoned, "Blessed be the One who is beneficent to the wicked and the good alike. Blessed is the One who has been beneficent to this granddaughter of Naftali, who has found her way to her family. And blessed be the One who has allowed us to raise this orphan girl in our home, the only one of our family left alive."

Our Master took the girl in and provided for all her needs—food, drink, lodging, clothing. Our Master, who was not particular about his own clothes except for his beautiful talit and tefillin, personally picked out the material for her dresses and personally sent for the cobbler to make her a pair of shoes. On Friday afternoons, before leaving for the bathhouse to get ready for the Sabbath, he would look in on the kitchen and ask, "Has she had her bath? Has her hair been combed?" Sometimes he would stand and make sure they were not hurting her when they combed her hair, which had gotten tangled during the long time in the forest.

As she grew older our Master thought about a match for her. He cast his eye on his favorite student, a clever and knowledgeable young man with some proficiency in several languages. This student was the son of Zevulun the spice merchant. Zevulun, after his death, left a manuscript of a book on the prayer recited upon embarking on a

journey. It contained some shocking things about disputations he had
with freethinkers in various cities in the Ottoman lands. I heard that
he had asked our Master to write an approbation for the book, and
our Master declined the invitation. He said that since the questions it
dealt with were of no concern to him, he was quite ready to forgo the
answers it offered.

So our Master married off Zlateh to Zevulun's son Aaron. Because
he loved the couple so much, our Master himself recited the seven nuptial benedictions at all seven wedding feasts. I remember that at the feast
of the seventh day they were sitting around the table and there was no
new guest present. The door opened and in came a young man with a
volume of the talmudic tractate Kiddushin in hand. And so they recited
the seven benedictions. Among the company was a scholar who loved to
joke. He said to Aaron, "You see, tractate Kiddushin itself has sent you
a new face so that all seven benedictions can be said."

About the young man who came in with tractate Kiddushin in hand I
have nothing to say. But about the tractate itself I do. I once saw in a certain book, *Kaftor vaferaḥ*, a tale about a scholar who spent his whole life
studying the tractate Ḥagigah. When he departed this world no one took
any notice, until there appeared a woman who lamented him loudly, the
way a bereaved wife keens for her husband. The woman was the tractate
Ḥagigah, which took on the form of a woman because of that scholar's
lifelong devotion to it.

Our Master made a place for the couple in his home and arranged
with Aaron fixed times to study Torah together, before dawn and at night
after the evening service. You had to see our Master sitting and learning
with him to know the love of a master for his student. Matters that our
Master would usually treat cursorily he expounded to him in minute
detail. Our Master saw in Aaron and Zlateh his aspirations for a new
generation that would serve God righteously in place of their parents
murdered by the enemy.

Suffering is hard, hard when it happens and hard afterward. Because
of the many troubles that had befallen the Jews, Aaron began to inquire

into what God had done to this people, into the great wrath that caused this people to be handed over to the Gentiles, Heaven forfend, to be destroyed by them.

One inquiry leads to another, like one mouse that squeals out to another until very soon a whole horde of them come and chew up all the clothing and household goods. Because of His love for us, God encumbers us with suffering in order to purge us of the qelipot we have acquired in the lands of the Gentiles and thereby prepare us for the day of His Redemption. But this young man reached the false conclusion that God had withdrawn His love from Israel.

Now when a person opens the door to speculation, if he is worthy he will repent, and God will bring him to inner peace, and nothing will unnerve him. Superior to him is one who never experiences any philosophical doubts. He will not be subverted by them; nor will he even have to expend intellectual energy to refute them. This young man, alas, was not worthy. His doubts were not only not dispelled, they multiplied. He became lax in his attitude to Torah and its observance. When he had the opportunity to perform a commandment, he did so not out of love or fear or religious yearning or because the Torah commanded him to do it. He did so only because the sources he was reading did not disapprove of it. When he studied Torah it was not with any love or holiness or because a Jew is enjoined to meditate upon it day and night. He studied Torah because it sharpens the intellect. How shameful, how disgraceful it is that there are people who think that the words of the living God are in need of human validation. And what is worse, they make the Torah secondary and human wisdom primary.

When a person studies Torah, the Torah protects him. When he does a commandment, the commandment saves him from transgression. But when he studies Torah and takes no joy in it, the Torah will take no joy in him. Torah and mitzvot will bring him only melancholy until perforce he will seek to anchor himself in something else. He will be oblivious to the fact that the qelipot created by his worthless investigations now encase him. Yet God's mercy is not exhausted, for were he to turn in repentance God would receive him. But contemptible ideas darkened his mind and prevented him from finding the doorway to repentance.

3

One day, an hour or two before dawn, our Master went to the beit midrash and did not find Aaron there. Our Master noticed me and asked me for an explanation. I said I would go and find out but he said, no, he would go himself. When Zlateh heard him coming she got out of bed and ran outside. "Where is Aaron?" our Master asked her. She went back to her room and found his bed just as she had made it the previous evening. Clearly he had not slept there. "Aaron is not here," she said, and fainted.

The Rabbi's wife heard about this and went to her, as did several neighbors, and eventually the whole town came. They all began to speculate and spin all kinds of tales, tales which were not so much implausible as improbable. When the speculation stopped, confusion set in. How could it be that the night before, he was seen in the synagogue, and in the morning he is gone? If he had started out for home after the evening service, did he disappear on the way? It was all quite baffling. Our Master seemed removed from the whole thing. Finally he bestirred himself and said, "It is time for the morning service."

The passing days brought little hope. All kinds of testimonies were offered, and rumors too. Our Master received the bearers of these rumors respectfully so as to keep people looking for new information. He spent a lot of time talking to the local peasants who, he knew, came to him only for the brandy he would give them. The more outlandish their talk, the more our Master paid attention to it. For example, a Gentile who had too much to drink told him of a Jew who burned a book revered by the Jews. Our Master sat there and hung on every word that came out of that Gentile's mouth.

Our Master could see the agony of his little relative who was not yet fifteen and was already an agunah. He put aside all his civic affairs and obligations and even his regular lectures on Maimonides and Alfasi and began to look into the matter of freeing this agunah. He had, apparently, abandoned all hope that Zlateh's husband would ever return. He searched for some ruling that would permit this woman to be freed from the chains of the marital bond. But no such ruling could he find.

Our Master, may the memory of the righteous be for a blessing, possessed prophetic powers that enabled him to divine that Aaron was dead. If he were alive, he reasoned, the law would be clear: it would be an open-and-shut case for all the rabbinical authorities and I would not even look for a way to permit her to marry where there is none. Furthermore, he ruminated, when I ponder the legal status of this poor girl, my heart and my head are divided. My head knows the law on the books while my heart tells me that maybe, or quite possibly, she is no agunah. Yet so long as no one comes forward to say that they saw him dead and buried, she remains a married woman plain and simple, and there is no way to declare her eligible to remarry. Can you imagine the compassion that saintly man had for this last surviving member of his family, a girl not yet fifteen who faced the prospect of living out her years as an agunah? No, his heart told him, her husband is dead. But what could he do? Neither a Gentile's idle talk nor a rabbi's prophetic powers are sufficient to free an agunah. Our Master conferred with all the illustrious rabbis of Poland and Lithuania, and not a single one of them could champion the cause of freeing this girl from her shackled state.

4

We are now at Monday morning of the week of the Torah portion *Behukotai*. Our Master is being called up to the Torah and I am helping him step up to the bimah. I looked at him and saw that he was in another world and struggling to get back to this one. I think to myself: he is trying to get his mind off that poor girl's predicament so he can concentrate on the blessings over the Torah.

After the reading, as I was helping him go down the steps and return to his place, he indicated that he wanted to tell me something. When he had taken off his tefillin, I went over to him. He looked up and said,

"Ah, here you are." He put his tefillin back in their bag, but he still had his talit on. He looked at me again and said to me these exact words: "I know that people do not frighten you. Go home and have breakfast and then come to me." Since he had instructed me to go home and eat, I felt no compulsion to stand there and wait for him to summon me.

I went home. My wife, may she rest in peace, was still alive then. While we were having breakfast she commented that I looked preoccupied. I wanted to tell her all that happened, but not everything one sees in the beit midrash has to be told to one's wife. I said to her, "I'm in a hurry now. Our Master is waiting for me."

"Why?"

"Maybe he wants me to deliver something for him."

She looked at me and said nothing. As I was leaving she said, "Do you remember that incident with the tax collector and the melamed?"

"Something like that you do not forget."

"That must be what is going on now. He wants you to deliver a message for him."

"If that is what it is, I would have been the first to know. Besides, a man is not banned by the community unless he has been summoned twice and refused to go both times. That tax collector paid for his sin in this world on top of what awaits him in the world to come. No one defies our Master. When he calls for his shamash, the shamash goes."

Now what was the story of the tax collector? There was a wealthy tax collector who hired a melamed to teach his son. The melamed toiled with the boy all winter. When it got to be spring and the month of Nissan was approaching, the melamed got ready to go home to his wife. He went to the tax collector to receive his wages. The tax collector, however, first wanted to examine the son to see what he had learned. He asked him if he knew how to say the kaddish. The boy could not. In fact, the boy had no idea of what the melamed had taught him, never mind what he had not. The tax collector became enraged at the melamed and paid him not a penny. The melamed stated yelling and screaming at him. "You want your payment?" said the tax collector. "Well here it is!" And he slapped him in the face. The melamed took the tax collector to the rabbinical court, but he did not show up. Our Master then instructed me to go and tell the man that if there is no legal accounting here below, there certainly is one up above, and if he would not appear before the local rabbinical court he would absolutely be hauled before the beit din of Gehinnom. So I went to him without the least fear of him or his dogs or his servants. I remarked to my wife that this story shows that if our Master himself fulfills the commandment in the Torah "*Fear no man*," even his assistants should be intimidated by no one. I said "his assistants" in the plural so that my wife would not be overly proud of me. Sometimes a wife's pride in her husband can make him haughty and arrogant.

I went back to our Master's house. He had been brought a cup of milk and a roll and taken off his pair of Rabbenu Tam's tefillin, which he gave to me to put away. He had never done that before. I surmised that our Master was feeling weak and was seeking to revive himself. He smiled and said, "Hah! How people forget. They sent me food." I realized that I, too, had forgotten that on Mondays and Thursdays our Master had the practice of fasting. But since one did not make small talk with our Master, I kept silent.

Then our Master said, "I would like to go to a certain place. Will you accompany me?" I was astounded. This great man whose company all seek is asking me to accompany him! If he asked me to go with him to Mountains of Darkness would I not go? Many times it seemed as though the look in his eyes told what he wanted to say to me. Our Master went on, "I want to go to a place where no living person ever goes. And should the attribute of justice begin to assert itself, the mercy of our blessed God will prevail."

Our Master saw that I was having a hard time understanding his meaning. So he sat down and explained. "I have gone as far as I could on behalf of the poor girl. The rabbinic authorities have all determined that she shall remain an agunah for the rest of her life. And since no witnesses have come forward to affirm that her husband is dead and buried, I want to find out for myself if he is living or dead."

I began to shake. I stood there trembling and aghast. Our Master reiterated, "If he is alive, he will surely repent. If he is dead, he is in Gehinnom, where all sinners in Israel descend. I will go there and see him. Will you go with me?"

I asked our Master which prayers I should say. He glanced at me and said, "A person should always feel as if the opening of Gehinnom were right underneath him. So when you pray you should feel as if you are standing on the very top of Gehinnom. The whole time you are praying it should feel as if these are the very last prayers you will utter in this world because you may never be given another chance. The grace of God allows us to pray but once in a lifetime. And what is that one and only time? That moment when you are standing in prayer." I then asked, "What should I have in mind during my prayer?" Our Master gazed at me and said, "Have in mind to keep your eyes open. If he is hiding from me and I do not see him, your eyes will be open to notice where he is."

5

On the Friday evening of the Sabbath of Repentance I went to our Master to ask him when he would give his discourse on repentance so that I could announce it. Truth be told, there really was no need to inquire. The normal order of things was that on the Sabbath of Repentance right after the midday meal, everyone would gather in the synagogue and recite psalms until the rabbi would get up to speak. But in those days nothing was done in our town without first asking our Master. I used to think that this was simply out of respect for him, until he once told me that all things require preparation in advance, especially repentance. A discourse on repentance certainly requires preparation of the heart. Our Master set the time. But right after I left him he called me back. I thought he was calling me back to tell me when we were departing for that place, I mean going to visit Gehinnom. He looked at me and said, "When you announce the time of my address, say in my name that people should be careful not to put up their Sukkah in an impure place."

This was a brand new directive that no rabbi had ever issued before, and he could see that it puzzled me. The rabbis of our town had never been concerned about this issue; nor for that matter had the rabbis of other communities. Our Master continued, "Our many sins compel us to live where we live and go where we go, and no one can be sure on what ground his feet are treading or where exactly he is standing. But a Sukkah, which epitomizes the mystery of the clouds of glory that God spread over Israel in the desert, requires a taintless spot on which to be erected, and we have to be very, very careful about that." When our Master said, "and go where we go" I had the feeling that we were already on the way to the place where the young agunah's husband was. Our Master gave me an approving look and indicated that our conversation was over.

On the way home I went over every word I had heard. How good it is to know that we have leaders whose words keep us on the straight path and sustain us in this Exile.

I came home and began making preparations for the Sabbath. Not only what was needed in the synagogue but at home as well, for my wife, may she rest in peace, was quite weak and could hardly stand on her feet. After the Sabbath I turned to Yom Kippur preparations. God's mercies were with us, because the holy day passed without incident. No one fainted from the fast, those who led the service did not stray from the proper melodies, the Torah reader made no mistakes in chanting the text. Not a single candle went out, neither those lit for the living nor those lit for the dead. There were so many candles that they all melted together. A great many people had perished in the slaughter and their surviving relatives lit candles in their memory. Our Master lit many for his own family. The only one left was that little girl now in limbo because of the sin her husband committed.

The next day I brought over to our Master the silver case in which he kept his etrog. Every year my first wife, may she rest in peace, would polish it in honor of the approaching festival. She always did this between Rosh Hashanah and Yom Kippur. That year, because she was not well, she waited until the day after Yom Kippur. This meant a change in our

Master's routine, for it was his custom in the evening, at the end of Yom Kippur after havdalah, to take out his etrog and put it in its case. Our Master did not even notice the change.

I entered to find him in the company of two men, the venerable magnate Reb Akiva Shas, so named because he was fortunate to own a complete set of the Talmud, and, like him distinguished in stature and character but not in wealth, Reb Meshullam, a Jew from Germany who was a descendant of the composer of the Akdamut hymn read on the festival of Shavuot. Old age had kept them from visiting the evening before, right after Yom Kippur, so they came the next day.

I put the etrog case down in front of our Master. He looked at it and remarked, "I understand your wife is in need of mercy from on high." "Yes," I said, "she is sick. And, thank God, we have a houseful of little children." I expected our Master to make some kind of blessing for her recovery, but he did not. Only later did I understand why. He knew what we did not: that her end had already been ordained. She died that year. Our Master then placed the etrog in the case and left the case open.

The etrog gave off its fragrance as our Master resumed reminiscing with his two elderly visitors about bygone days, and in due course he told a story that, in the particular context, was disconcerting. There was a time when for many years etrogs were scarce and people began to worry that Jews would soon forget what an etrog was. One year, between Rosh Hashanah and Yom Kippur, two Jews from a distant country showed up with etrogs for sale. The community bought one at a very steep price. No one seemed to care that the community was mired in debt, having borrowed money from the local priests to ransom prisoners. Many doubted that the etrog was kosher or if one could even make the blessing over it. Nevertheless, everyone did, even the doubters, because the commandment to bless the etrog was very dear to them. After the Sukkot festival someone got the idea that the etrog should be examined. Everyone came to see. They cut it open and discovered that it was in fact a lemon, which meant that all the blessings made over it were in vain. Around Passover time, when the snow was melting, two corpses were found in the forest. Wolves had eaten them and nothing was left but bones and clothing. The clothing was examined and found to be that of the men who had sold the etrog. Whom to suspect of their murder? Not Jews, for even if they had known that the men had sold them a lemon instead of an etrog they would not have committed murder. Not God, for God does not execute judgment unjustly. They convened a beit din to look into the legal status of the wives of the dead men. Were they agunot or did the clothing found prove them to be widows? The question became moot when the wicked Khmelnitski's pogroms erupted and many women were taken into captivity, including the widows of the etrog sellers.

Once his two visitors had gone, our Master showed me the passage in the talmudic tractate 'Eruvin where it says that Gehinnom has three openings: one in the desert, one in the sea, and one in Jerusalem. He also showed me another passage there that says that Gehinnom has seven names, and he explained to me the fine points of the differences between them. He concluded by telling me that since the destruction of Jerusalem not every wicked person has the merit of going down to Gehinnom from the opening that is in Jerusalem. For the majority of the wicked, Gehinnom opens right at their feet, under their very feet. He then taught me some laws relating to Gehinnom. But there was no mention of a visit there.

That night after the evening service I could see that our Master was staring at me. I went over to him but he said nothing. I stood and looked at him and saw that his face was burning and his white curls were glistening with sweat. Because of headaches that resulted from a sword wound, our Master never cut his hair, not even for Yom Kippur.

I stood before him but he paid no attention to me. I did not move. I thought to myself, he is not looking at me like that for no reason. He continued staring at me, when he said, "Take the lantern and let us set out." Even though he did not say where we were going, I knew. Of course, when he said "let us set out" his actual words were "In the name of God, let us go." I do not quote his exact words because any intelligent person knows that nothing is done without asking for God's help first. Happy is he who asks and happy is he who is answered.

I now return to the main story.

I had with me candles made from the wax that dripped from the ones lit in the synagogue on Yom Kippur. I normally used them on Hoshana Rabba and on the twentieth of Sivan. In our Master's time people did not run to catch the wax drippings from the Yom Kippur candles right after the concluding evening prayer. They were too intent on greeting our Master and getting a blessing from him. So the wax was mine for the taking. I took all the candles I had with me so that darkness would not engulf us if the journey would prove to be a long one. When a person is alive he cannot see that the pit of Gehinnom is open right in front of him. He goes on his way and has no idea that it is right in front of him. I put the candle into the lantern but had no need to light it, for all this happened between Yom Kippur and Sukkot and it was a bright night.

We went out to the courtyard of the synagogue. Our Master stood and checked the direction of the wind. He sniffed the breeze, got his bearings, and said, "Let us go."

We passed the synagogues and came out behind the Strypa at the Butchers Street. From there we got to Ox Gore Street, so named because an ox once gored a woman and her children there. Today it is called King Street. From there we headed northwest.

As long as we were in the town our Master would take one step and stop, one step and stop. It seemed as if it was hard for him, as if he had almost forgotten how to walk. He never went outside more than twice a year, once to draw the water for making matzot and once on Rosh Hashanah to perform the tashlikh ritual. And if the first day of Shavuot was clear, he would go out to the surrounding hills to commemorate the giving of the Torah at Mt. Sinai. You can still see the rock on which he would sit and rest.

The moon shone and all was still. In the silence every so often we could hear the sound of hammering. People were putting up their sukkot. Once or twice our Master stopped to whisper the words "Hark! My beloved knocks." I knew that his whole reason for stopping was to take in the sight of all those sukkot. He remembered the terrible years when people were hiding from Khmelnitski's hordes and no one could observe the commandment of dwelling in the sukkah.

Once we got beyond town the moon disappeared and the road became rugged. I quickly lit the candle and held on to the lantern tightly. It felt as if someone were trying to grab it away from me. At times I thought I heard someone trying to blow out the candle though there was no wind. And it seemed as if someone was whispering in my ear, though I could not hear what it was. I got an earache from those murmurings. My fingers were shaking from holding on to the lantern so tightly.

We walked on in silence. When our Master was quiet, I was too. No one ever dared speak in his presence unless he gave them permission— that is how much respect we had for him. How far we walked I cannot say. Once we left the town I lost all track of time. I became numb with fear. If our Master had not motioned for me to take hold of the hem of his cloak, I would have died of fright. At first I thought he had some amulets with him, but when I heard him whispering, "Though I walk through the valley of the shadow of death, I fear no evil, for Thou art with me," then I knew that he put his trust in the Eternal One, in Him alone, may He be blessed.

6

Were I to tell of all the difficulties our Master and I had on the way, I would never finish. Were I to recount all the places we passed, I would never get to the site of this story. Our Master extracted me from the domain of space just as he had taken me out of the flow of time. Much later, when I got back from where we had gone, all the places we passed through came back to me. They swirl before me even now, sometimes all jumbled together, sometimes hovering dimly on the ravines of hills and mountains, the sky above them lowering. The space between heaven and earth is as thin as an eggshell. Sometimes the earth rears itself up and presses against the sky, and sometimes the blue dome of the heavens takes on the dark color of the earth below. When I stand here, down below, it feels as though I am there, up above, and when I stand there, up above, it feels like I am here, down below. But enough of this.

The shamash proceeded:

Those who think that a wicked person who dies goes down to Gehinnom do not know that there is a punishment even more severe. It is known as "being hurled from the hollow of the sling." This sling punishment is not a place, as the treatises have it, but a bloody brawl, so named because of what is done to the sinners. They are so battered by the embroilments of their sins that they try to seek refuge in Gehinnom. But no sooner do they approach its gates than they are flung back to all the places where they sinned and where they thought about sinning. But now they cannot find those places because the sins committed there have disfigured them, and the ones that are still recognizable crumble underfoot, and sharp spikes spring up and impale their soles. Snarling dogs appear and nip at their heels. Some of these sinners are encrusted with soil, and when they are flung the soil is hurled and they remain suspended in midair. Some return to the gates of Gehinnom, while others never arrive there again.

A sinner's punishment, then, is hard, but even worse is what happens to someone who wants to sin but does so only in thought and not in deed. Someone who has actually sinned is to some extent cleansed by the remorse, suffering and heartbreak he will feel. But one who wanted to sin and never had the chance to do so will be undone by the prideful illusion that he knows how to control himself even as the fires of temptation still burn within him. Worst of all are those contemptible people who feel false pangs of conscience and fancy that they have repented, yet all the while they are consumed by sinful thoughts and their illusory pleasures. No one can accuse me of loving sinners, but when I see them flung around like that, I am quite ready to hire myself out as the doorkeeper of Gehinnom so I can personally let them in.

The shamash proceeded:

There are distinguished people who think that after they die they will go straight to Gan Eden. But when I visited Gehinnom with our Master I saw that it was filled with such people. Let me be more precise about this. Those who fill the ranks of Gehinnom are people who have already attained considerable merit. Those who have not descend to the nethermost parts of Sheol, which is to Gehinnom as Gehinnom is to Gan Eden. I mention no names here out of respect for their families. In this regard I try to emulate a practice our Master instituted after he came back from Gehinnom. Before he went, his study was focused on the Zohar and the writings of the Ari, aside from the regular classes he gave in halakhah. When he came back he devoted himself to studying Mishnah. The Mishnah study was for the purpose of raising up the souls of those who went down to Gehinnom, even though everyone thought they were righteous while they were alive. I try to do likewise. Though I am poor, whenever I get penny from the children and grandchildren of such people, I light a candle in their memory.

7

When the shamash finished these digressions, he resumed his story, first telling about the husband who abandoned his wife, then recounting all the twists and turns of the journey, then relating all the extraordinary things he had seen—everything that led up to and resulted from the fact that he had thrown a scholar from a prominent family out of the beit midrash for talking during the Torah reading.

I remove myself from the narrative and take on the character of the shamash so he can speak in his own voice. But lest you start thinking that this story is about me, I intrude periodically with the words "the shamash said."

And so he did, as follows:

Look how modest our Master was, may the memory of the righteous be for a blessing: he had taken me with him to serve as his spotter, yet it was he who recognized the wicked one first. When Aaron realized he had been seen, he ran over to our Master and said, "Rebbe, you are here! I always knew you would come to me. When a scholar goes into exile, his master is exiled with him." Our Master nodded. "Tractate Makkot folio 10a, a little below the middle of the page!" Our Master, may the memory of the righteous be for a blessing, always did that. Whenever someone quoted a passage from the Talmud he would think for a moment and then cite the tractate, the folio, the precise side of the folio— a or b—and sometimes even the exact line and whether it was on the top half of the page or the bottom half of the page. The two of them began to converse quietly.

Our Master said to Aaron, "How could you leave your wife, the woman you married according to the laws of Moses and Israel? You transgressed, but what about your wife? What was her sin that you made not the least effort to release her from the shackles of her chained state? How terrible it is that your sin has wiped out your capacity for mercy, which is the hallmark of a Jewish person."

At this Aaron let out a wail and began crying loudly and bitterly. "They never let me! They never let me to go to her! They buried me in their cemetery, a Gentile cemetery with a cross on my grave! Two sticks, vertical and horizontal. They cut me off from Jews, and I had no way to get to a Jewish home. When I wanted to leave my grave to visit my wife in a dream and tell her that I was dead and that she was free to remarry, the cross would bar my way, and I could not get to her. Rebbe, Gehinnom is terrible, but the torment of knowing that I left my wife to be an agunah is much, much worse."

I could see tears in our Master's eyes. I heard him ask, "My son, how did you get here? For what sin did you die?" I heard Aaron's answers and got the gist of what he said, but I was so terror-stricken that I do not remember his exact words. But I do remember the gist of it. If there is a difference here between what he said and what I report, it is not in the content. He spoke in the first person, the technical term for which is "indirect speech." I give over his words in the third person. He spoke, he cried, he spoke, he groaned, he sighed, and I was as one who heard it all from afar.

When Aaron saw the troubles that had overtaken Israel, he began to wonder about what God had done to this people and what lay behind this great and terrible anger. He started to probe the matter deeply but found no answers. He immersed himself in volumes of theosophical speculation, the great texts of the Kabbalah, the *Kanah* and the *Peli'ah*. Now a man who is righteous and along in years will read such texts and attain an even deeper sense of awe. But a young man wet behind the ears who starts delving into Kabbalah will bring upon himself only inner turmoil, all the more so when he fills his head with metaphysical investigations. He will not only fail to grow in piety, he will fall into the depths of the qelipot. That is what happened to Aaron. He not only failed to resolve his doubts, he reached the dire conclusion that the God of Israel had disengaged Himself from Israel, Heaven forbid, and had become, Heaven forbid, an enemy.

As the saying goes, "One who seeks to purify himself will get help from above, just as one who seeks to pollute himself will find the door open to him." Foolishly, Aaron decided to find out what the Gentile scholars say. He took the trouble to learn Latin and picked up in one year what the priests could not learn in seven. He buried his nose in their books and pored over their words, but the ideas he found there brought him no satisfaction. And sure enough, when a person loses his way, Satan comes and leads him on.

Satan showed him the way to a priest. Those priests have books that deal with what is above and what is below and what came before and what will be in the end, and they put forth ridiculous ideas that do nothing to resolve doubts about those matters. They say, for example, that when the different languages originated after the Tower of Babel, God created strange creatures with swordlike hands with which they incised letters in their books. Some of those books were written under the sign of Mars, and their guardian angel was Gabriel. That is totally false. Gabriel loves the Jews and champions their cause. Some of those books were written under the sign of Venus and were protected by the daughters of humans who were corrupted by the superhuman sons of God. That is a bit closer to the truth but needs to be qualified, because one of the maidens separated herself from transgression and ascended to the firmament to become one of the stars of the Pleiades. The priests bind all their books in pigskin, and as they read them the light in their soul darkens until eventually they fall into tehom, the abyss which is hinted at in the verse *and darkness was over the surface of the deep*. And note: the word tehom is made up of the same four Hebrew letters as the word hamavet (Death), and the two are one and the same, which is why tehom is the domain of the qelipot.

Aaron borrowed a few books from the priest and secreted himself away with them as one would with an adulterous woman. He drank of the bitter water, and the bitter water induced its curse within him. A person possesses two souls, an outer one that encompasses him about, and an inner one. When a person sins, God forbid, his inner soul descends below while he is still in this life.

One Friday night Aaron was at home alone. Zlateh had gone off to search for her father's grave. As you know, her father disappeared just after the murder of his father-in-law Reb Naftali. Both deaths occurred right before the pogroms of 1648–49 and were forgotten in the ensuing carnage.

It so happened that a Jewish butcher from our town made a trip to a certain place to buy cattle. A Gentile there started bragging about his cows, which, he said, were of superior quality because they grazed in a field where Jews were buried. On hearing this, the butcher pretended not to believe him. So the Gentile called his mother, who related how she had worked in the home of Naftali the wine merchant and how his son-in-law worked with him in the business. One day Naftali came to the estate in a wagon loaded with casks of wine. When night fell he slept in the open next to his wagon. Now the lord of the estate had some young noblemen who regularly dined with him. They caught the scent of the wine, went out and opened all the casks, and proceeded to get good and drunk. When they sobered up they became fearful that the lord would punish them, because he had promised the authorities that no harm would come to merchants passing through his estates. Besides, they knew that with a nobleman of his stature no actions were to be taken without his orders. After debating what to do, they killed the wine merchant. They knew it was likely that some nobleman would inform on them. After all, noblemen informed on Jews and were just as likely to inform on them. So they took the body and buried it in a field where there were Jewish graves from long ago. When Zlateh heard about all this she went with the butcher's wife to find her father's grave. But she got delayed and could not get back before the Sabbath.

That night Aaron dined with our Master. After dinner he went home and forgot that it is forbidden to sleep in one's house all alone. Why, you may ask, did our Master not remind him about that? He assumed that Aaron had arranged for a Yeshiva student to come over and stay with him overnight. So Aaron went home, sat down, and read through the weekly Torah portion. When he finished and then reviewed the prophetic reading, he found a verse in it that troubled him. He reviewed the commentaries but found no explanation that satisfied him. He then went to see what the Christian exegetes had to say. From under his bed he took out one of the books the priest had loaned him and started reading but could not make out a single letter. He thought that this was because the candle was set down too low. He did not know that on the holy Sabbath Jewish eyes cannot take in anything written in Gentile script.

One whose punishment already awaits him will forget that it is Sabbath, as Aaron did that night. He got up and took the candle and placed it on top of one of the Christian books and sat and read. Satan then did his work and Aaron's eyes did theirs. He went on reading until the candle burned down without his noticing. The candle burned through the book it was sitting on, leaving a round hole in the middle. When Aaron later returned the book, the priest took one look at it and promptly accused him of deliberately setting fire to it. He threatened to have Aaron drawn and quartered and thrown to the dogs, but if he accepted the Christian faith he could be saved. Furthermore, they would spare him all the suffering the Jews were facing, and if he feared retribution from them, the priest would arrange for him to be taken to a place where there were no Jews and no fear of Jews. Aaron chose life over death and thus bartered eternal life for this transient one. In his heart he fantasized escaping to another country, returning to the God of Israel, and getting word to his wife to come and join him. Fearing that the Gentiles would somehow discover his designs, he redoubled his violations of Jewish practice so as to show them that he accepted their god with a perfect faith. But he was torn up inside. He began to afflict his body by fasting, even though he knew that fasting without repentance is of no avail. His body shriveled and the volume of his blood shrank, not only from the fasting but also from the agony he suffered. At length he took sick and died. They buried him in a Gentile cemetery and put a cross on his grave, thereby setting up a permanent barrier between him and the Jews and preventing him from visiting his wife in a dream to inform her that he was dead and she could remarry. When a Jew engages in idolatry it is as if the idolatry itself is empowered to do him harm.

That is the story of Aaron. But I must add here something that I really should have stated earlier. That year, on the Sabbath of Repentance before we went on the journey to Gehinnom, our Master began his discourse with these words: "Preachers who chastise their congregations customarily begin with a verse from the weekly Torah portion and conclude with the verse *And a redeemer shall come to Zion and to those in Jacob who turn from transgression, says the Lord.* I, however, shall begin with that verse. *And a redeemer shall come to Zion* summarizes the foundation of our faith and the basis of repentance, for when we see year after year the same tribulations, and we continue to wait for the End of Days, and we are not destroyed by the Gentiles—all that gives us the strength and the courage to turn in complete repentance." That is what I mean when I say that our Master possessed the power of prophesy. Because even before he spoke with Aaron in Gehinnom, he already knew that his sin consisted in his having questioned the very idea of an End of Days.

That is the story of Aaron, husband of Zlateh, and it is through his fate that I came to see how severe is the punishment for all who talk during the service and the Torah reading.

If this introduction is longer than the story, more severe still is the story itself. I wish I were not telling it, and now that I am telling it, I hope it will not be taken as just a story but rather that you will learn from it how very careful we must be not to talk in the synagogue during the prayers and especially during the reading of the Torah.

8

Aaron's story diverted everyone's attention from the shamash's case, and it was the shamash himself who brought them back to it. "If you wish to hear it," he said, "I will now tell it. But I must add a word or two before I begin."

The shamash sat upright and a great sadness emanated from him. It created a wall between him and the assembled. If he had not begun speaking, no one would have reminded him that they wanted to hear the story he was about to relate.

This is what he said:

I know that I have violated the teachings of our Sages according to which one who embarrasses another person in public forfeits his share in the world to come. Not only have I violated that teaching, I have impugned the honor of a scholar of good family and the son-in-law of a benefactor of the community, whose generosity underwrites half the expenses of our synagogue; moreover, I have shamed him not for mindless chatter but for talking Torah, and doing that not in a Gentile marketplace but in a holy place in front of the Torah scroll, and on the holy Sabbath, when the Holy One spreads the tent of peace over Israel. I have therefore every right to regret what I did. But not only do I have no regret, I am certain that when I die, a band of beneficent angels will come out to welcome me saying, Come, let us keep company with someone who selflessly relinquished his share in the world to come in order to save another person from a harsh sentence and severe punishment. I could cite sources for my position in our holy books, but there are present here learned men who have the whole Torah at their fingertips. So I will simply tell you what my eyes saw. Solomon the wise wrote that *What the eyes see is better than the flights of desire.* He means to say that what a person sees with his own eyes is better than where his fancy takes him. His fancy roams over mountain tops, descends into valleys, creeps into caves, and insists that the earth is flat.

From what you have heard about Aaron so far, you know that our Master, may the memory of the righteous ever be for a blessing, took me to that place. I cannot tell you all that I saw there. Nor do I want to tell you all that I saw there. But I can speak of some of the things these ancient eyes saw when they were younger.

I pass over all the old man's moanings and groanings and "oy vays" and get to the main events. At some points I will cite him word for word, at others I will paraphrase, and at some points I will summarize. But I must note that even though the shamash was rather long-winded about the events surrounding Aaron, which was after all only a prologue, when it came to the events themselves he was concise. I have found that it is easier to relate what you have heard from others than to relate what your own eyes have seen. It was easier for the old man to tell what he heard from Aaron than to recount what he himself had seen. In any case, being succinct will not diminish the story.

I will mark off his words from mine by prefacing them with the phrase "the shamash said," except now, where it will be obvious that he is speaking.

9

In Gehinnom there is a compartment they call Tsalmavet, Shadow of Death. It is larger than Earth in size, and its dimensions are perfectly symmetrical. Nothing in the world is as paradoxical as that compartment. It is circular in shape but appears square, square in shape but appears circular. The eyes perceive it one way, the mind another. These differences in perspective induce a certain melancholy.

In that compartment it is neither hot nor cold nor in-between. No wind blows there, only an occasional vapid gust encased in a cool dry silent breeze. A nameless long-legged angel oversees the compartment, but this angel does absolutely nothing. It stands there with its mouth agape, like a person utterly bored and about to yawn.

The compartment is populated by twice the number of people who went out of Egypt, all of them wrapped in silver-crowned talitot. The tefillin on their heads are as big as those worn by chief rabbis and heads of yeshivot. The space between one person and another is equivalent to the distance of a Sabbath boundary. All of them are brilliant intellects with a profound knowledge of Talmud and its earlier and later authorities. Each one sits by himself, in talit and tefillin, steeped in Torah. When he seeks to disseminate his wisdom, he looks this way and that but sees no one. The years of poring over tomes of text have dimmed his eyes and he is unable to notice that there are thousands upon thousands of Torah scholars just like him there. Boastfully he thinks, "I'm all alone in the world; all wisdom dies with me." He gets up from his place, looks around and sees a multitude of people as tiny as sesame seeds. He says to himself, "The tefillin on their heads tell me that they are human beings, so I will go over to them and say a pilpul." But then he becomes drowsy and falls asleep, like a hermaphrodite who sleeps without pleasure or desire or satisfaction or sweet dreams, until he awakens and doesn't know if he is really awake or has simply turned over on his side. He notices a humanlike form striding by and gets up and walks toward it. When the two draw near, one of them says, "I have developed a brand new pilpul no one has ever thought of before." The other replies, "You are taking the words right out of my mouth. The pilpul that I have devised every bone in your body would strain to hear. But since you desire to speak, I defer to you. And now, since I have deferred to you, it would be right for you too to defer your desire to speak to mine. Moreover, since I deferred to you before you deferred to me, it follows that I should rightfully have primacy. Therefore, I should speak first." As soon as he begins to speak his mouth grows as wide as a church courtyard. His colleague says,

"A pilpul like that just goes right past me." At which point his ears grow bigger and bigger until they cover his whole body. The two of them stand there gaping at each other, confounded, frightened, ready to scream. But no scream is heard from either one. The first one's scream dies in his throat, and the other's is muffled by his ears. At that moment the angel sways from side to side, the only time it ever moves. It sits and gazes at the two of them as if they were one, looking not with its eyes but with its mouth. If the angel had not then wanted to yawn, that look would have killed them.

10

I place the different punishments described here in different chapters so as to separate them, even though the shamash recounted them without interruption, except when he gave forth with such anguished expressions as "oy vay!" and various invocations of God and His mercies.

Just as he went on uninterruptedly, so did his listeners never cease being amazed at what they were hearing. They knew full well that a righteous person goes to Gan Eden and a wicked person to Gehinnom and that there are certain righteous ones who enter Gan Eden while still alive. But in all their days they had never heard of anyone who went into Gehinnom alive and came out unscathed—until they heard from that old gentleman that he himself saw Gehinnom in his lifetime and walked around inside it as one walks around in his home, and even the hems of his clothing were not singed. You might think that this was because he was great in Torah and wisdom and piety and good deeds. Not at all. This was a poor shamash, one who was no different from anyone else in Buczacz, except for his temper. Perhaps the merits of his forebears who were killed in the pogroms stood in his stead. But in this matter he was no more privileged than the other townspeople, almost all of whom saw their father or mother die a terrible and cruel death. So the matter is truly puzzling.

Many things are unfathomable. I can shed no light on them and therefore return to the main thread of this tale, continuing again with the phrase "the shamash went on."

11

The shamash went on:

Beneath that compartment of Gehinnom is another one known as Gag 'al Gag, Roof Upon Roof. It is several times bigger than the first one and wider. It is so wide, in fact, that the walls, the ceiling, and the floor are invisible to the naked eye. It is as if the whole compartment were suspended over the void. Of course the earth too is suspended over the void, but the earth, as the Bible says, He has given to mankind, which means that the earth was given by God to mankind so it could flourish over the void. But in the nothingness over which this place hangs nothing can flourish. The people sitting here all have foreheads that are either wide or high or wrinkled. Their eyes are small, squeezed by all the intellectual activity into the space between the forehead and the nose. Some of them stroke their beards, some of them pluck out hair after hair and flick them into the air without even knowing it. This part of Gehinnom is different from the first; there the people sit as far from each other as the distance of a Sabbath boundary, whereas here they sit right next to each other, cramped together, each one sharing his ḥidush with the other, exactly as they did in the land of the living. The name of the angel appointed over them is Otem. This is not Gabriel, who covers over Israel's sins with a veil, but an evil angel who once was good but was debased by all the silly ḥidushim he heard. All this I learned from what our Master, may the memory of the righteous be for a blessing, told me.

The people here do exactly what they did when they were alive, namely, they offer ḥidushim anywhere and anytime. The difference is that in this world a person who recognizes that he is mistaken will, if he so chooses, admit his error, or if he is so inclined will deny it completely. There every word a person uttered in this world is permanently engraved in public view with his signature attached, and the dead cannot contradict what the living say.

When a person studies a page of Talmud and parses the plain sense of the text, the more his reading approximates what the words say, the less will he seek out colleagues to praise him for it. But when a person thinks up a ḥidush on that text, the more far-fetched it is, the more eager he is to proclaim it. He leans over to his colleague to propose it to him and his lips fly apart. His tongue goes in search of his lips and becomes impaled on the sharp edges of his teeth, whereupon it starts to swell, growing thicker and thicker. I am an old man and do not like exaggerations, but when I say that that tongue becomes as massive as a church bell I would not be too far from the truth. My comparison to a church bell is apt, for just as a church bell peals without knowing why, so the tongue wags without knowing why it was put into motion. His colleague sees all this and starts to yell, but no sound comes forth. I am an old man and have seen much trouble and travail, but misery like that I have never seen.

I buried my face in our Master's cloak so that I would not have to look at all that suffering. I covered my eyes but the torments were still visible. I stood there wondering: what offense brought on such a punishment?

12

I reviewed all the sins and punishments enumerated in the holy books and could find none that matched what I had seen—and the mercies of the Heavenly One are presumably greater than those of mortal men. Panic seized me. Maybe *my* mouth was contorted. Maybe *my* lips had flown apart. I was afraid to raise my hands to check. And then I feared that ears had grown over my whole body. When fear takes hold of a person, nature then compounds it. Because I had buried my face in the folds of our Master's cloak, I suddenly felt as if my ears were wrapped all around me. If I told you that I heard all the bones in my body rattling, it would not be far from the truth.

Our Master turned and looked back at me. My head cleared for a moment, and I wanted to ask him about the meaning of the forms we had just seen. But I had no voice. I vowed then that if I could ever talk again, I would make sure that not one unnecessary word would come out of my mouth.

Our Master continued to observe me. He was trying to determine just how much I could stand to hear. He was always very careful to adjust what he said to the capacity of his listeners. Rabbi Yitzhak the Chastiser once told me about a goldsmith named Reb Moshe of Buczacz. He told it in the name of his father Reb Yedidiah Lieberman, the nephew of Rabbi Mikhl of Nemirov, may God avenge his blood, who heard it in the name of the holy Rabbi Shimshon of Ostropol, may God avenge his blood. Reb Moshe was a goldsmith, and he once received precious stones and pearls from the king's vault to make a pair of earrings for the princess. He calibrated the earrings according to the weight her ears could bear.

Our Master kept on looking at me and then said, "What were you asking?" He wanted to see how important my question was to me. Sometimes the mouth wants to ask more than the heart wants to know. I did not dare ask, but the desire to know gnawed at me. The question was evident in my eyes, as when someone raises his eyes quizzically. Our Master paused for a moment and then said, "The people that you saw are all illustrious men. Some of them are rabbis, some are heads of yeshivot, some are officials, leaders, and regional rabbis. It is because of their stature that they have their own compartment of Gehinnom." He added, "The wicked in Gehinnom are punished with the very sin for which they were found guilty. The people you saw are punished with the opposite of what they committed. Because they sinned by speech, they are condemned to be mute."

Here our Master stopped and pointed to the lantern I was holding. I looked and saw that the candle was about to burn out. I quickly pulled out another one and lit it with the one that was reaching its end, sticking the new one on top of the old.

Seeing this, our Master recited the verse *The soul of man is a candle of the Lord.* He always paused a bit when he quoted a Biblical verse so as to set it apart from his own speech. Then he said to me, "Some candles shine right to their end and even as they go out they burn brightly. And some candles go out while still burning. Happy is the one whose soul shines forth in this world and its light continues on in the world to come. Now, as for what you asked me, the people you saw sitting far apart sat right next to each other in their lifetime, and all the synagogues and study houses were filled with their talk. Now they cannot utter a word, not because they are dead but because they chattered during prayers and nattered while the Torah was being read. Though they are allowed to devise ḥidushim, they are punished thus: when they wish to present their ḥidushim to others, their lips fly apart and their tongues are impaled on their teeth. Their colleagues see this and start to scream, but the sound dies in their mouths."

Our Master added, "The people you saw are not new arrivals. Among them are scholars who have been sitting there for generations, some from before the expulsion from Spain, some even from the time of the Talmud. Happy is he whose transgression is forgiven. But there is one sin about which the Holy One, blessed be He, is very particular, and that is talking during the service and the Torah reading. God Himself is truly compassionate and gracious and forgives iniquity, but the angels created by transgressions are an unforgiving lot. Happy is he who does not talk while praying. His prayer ascends to the Gates of Mercy and becomes a crown for his Creator."

13

Our Master's words disturbed me more than anything my eyes had seen. I knew that talking during prayers and Torah reading is a serious offence, but I had no idea how serious.

I was mortified. Who can say that he has never committed that sin? Who among us keeps his lips and tongue under control at all times? Who has not talked during the service or the Torah reading? And if those learned in Torah bear such a punishment, what about the rest of us? Even if the ḥidushim that scholars come up with do not always spring from the purest motives, there is still a scintilla of sincerity behind them. May you good people of Buczacz never know the dread I was feeling.

Adding to my anxiety was my astonishment at the duration of the punishment. Can that be the penalty for talking during the service or Torah reading? Even if one could explain it as the consequence of the bother the angels had to go to in separating true prayers from idle talk, the matter still remains unsettled and unsettling.

A verse in the Torah occurred to me: *The sword shall not cross through your land.* I interpreted *the sword* to refer to metaphysical speculation, and the verse to be saying that as it passes through your mind it will not only not undermine your faith, it could even strengthen it. In my heart I recited the verse *I am racked with grief, sustain me in accordance with Your word.* Our Master looked at me and whispered, "It is time to go back." My heart broke within me and I followed him.

Here the shamash suddenly stopped to survey the room. After he took in with one glance a group of scholars, his eye caught sight of some others who were not learned but who had a voice in civic affairs. While he was still looking around he continued:

Now listen to me all you people of Buczacz. You think that Gehinnom is only for Torah scholars. Well, let me tell you otherwise. There is one area there compared to which all the rest of Gehinnom is like Gan Eden. I never noticed it at first because it was covered in dust. But the voices that could be heard through the dust suggested that there were people there. I could not tell if they were people or cattle or fowl until I went in and saw that it was one huge market fair, like the ones our great-grandparents and those who came before them used to tell about, before Khmelnitski, may his name be blotted out. There were traders, dealers, noblemen and noblewomen, goods galore—like you've never seen before. Silver and gold and all kinds of expensive things. Then suddenly the whole fair was thrown into a panic. The Tatars had arrived. They came on swift horses in rumbling hordes. My body trembles even now as I recall it. I will stop talking about it and go back to where I left off.

So our Master was looking at me and said, "We have to go." My heart broke within me, but I followed him.

The earth was drenched in dew and the firmament moist with the perspiration generated by the stars in their efforts to illumine the world. The whole way along, our Master said not one word. Was he ruminating about Aaron's death, or about liberating the young agunah from her bonds? Who am I to say? Once or twice our Master looked up at the heavens and I could hear him whisper, "The stars are bunched together like a brood of chicks under a hen." Truthfully, I have no idea if he really said that or if I just thought he did. Because on the eve of Yom Kippur, at first light, when I went into the chicken coop to get the atonement chickens for my wife and me, may she rest in peace, I saw chicks roosting under the mother hen and I was reminded of a line in the Book of the Angel Razi'el, "many stars are clustered together like chicks under a hen." And so when I saw our Master look upward and whisper, those words came to me. By the time the sun rose, we were back in the courtyard of the synagogue.

Our Master kissed the mezuzah and then placed his walking stick in the courtyard behind the door and the mezuzah. I really should have taken it from him, but our Master never let anyone help him with his walking stick. After all, when Samson was blind he never asked anyone to get his staff for him in all his twenty-two years of judging Israel, and the Sages praised him for that. Our Master always took his stick and put it back by himself. But whenever he went to the sink to wash his hands, I would go and place it right near him so he would not have to bend down to get it.

He washed his hands, dried them and with his customary humility recited the Torah blessings in his sweet voice. I am not among those who claim to know what goes on in Heaven, but I am reasonably sure that when our Master said those blessings, each one was answered with an "Amen" from on high.

When he was seated in his usual place, I went over to him to ask him who should lead the morning service. In his day no one ever approached the lectern to lead unless our Master himself gave him permission to do so. He asked whether there was anyone present who had an obligation to lead, such as a man observing yahrzeit. Before I could answer he told me to go up.

I put on my talit and tefillin and went up to the Ark. I am an old man and I do not like to exaggerate, but I can tell you that I felt as if my feet were standing on the roof of Gehinnom and that this was the very last prayer that I would be allowed to utter. Miracle of miracles, I was still alive when the service ended.

That day I went to a scribe to have him check my tefillin to see if perhaps some letter on the parchment inside had faded. The fear and anxiety I had felt during the trip made me perspire so profusely that it was possible that the parchment had been affected. Praise be the One who crowns Israel in glory, not a single letter was spoiled.

When the service was over I brought the talmudic tractate Yevamot to our Master. He looked at me and said, "Sukkot is approaching. In honor of this festival of our joy, let us delight ourselves with tractate Sukkah." I went and got it for him and remained standing there. If he needed me he would see that I was at his disposal. He acknowledged this with a nod and told me to return home.

On the way I began to have doubts about whether the things I had seen were real or a dream. If I were to go by our Master's behavior, it may very well have been a dream, because normally he would have the talmudic tractate Yevamot on his desk, and here he was looking at tractate Sukkah. Furthermore, if that was truly Gehinnom that I saw, there were no flames. And even if you say that the judgment of wicked in Gehinnom lasts for twelve months, it is known that the fires of Gehinnom never go out. I also saw nothing of the snow in which the wicked are frozen. The pain is supposed to be worse than the heat of the sun.

At home I found no rest. I was worried that my wife would ask me where I had been all night. But she did not, presuming I had been in bed the whole night. Her illness had gotten worse, and she had lost the power of speech. If it had not been for the power of intuition, I would not have known when to feed her and take care of her.

14

My doubts intensified about whether I was awake when I saw those visions. When I returned to the beit midrash, I had the distinct impression that I had seen a number of the bluebloods of the congregation the previous night in all three compartments of Gehinnom. I knew it was not them I had seen but their fathers and grandfathers. Sons usually resemble their fathers or their grandfathers, and I had known all of them. My confusion distracted me from my prayers, and I knew it was my punishment for presuming that such decent people could be in Gehinnom.

I tried to stop thinking about those visions, but I could not. If I had not been distracted by my wife's worsening condition, I do not know what would have been with me.

One could not have guessed that our Master, may the memory of the righteous be for a blessing, was about to do something momentous, namely, free a young agunah from the chains of her condition by dint of the fact that we saw her dead husband in Gehinnom. I had often thought to myself, he has to do that or all the arduous efforts he put himself through to make the journey there would have been for naught.

The righteous do what they do and God does what He does. One day just before Ḥanukah, a man from a distant country appeared. He was strangely dressed, his round beard neatly trimmed, and his brownish hair had no sidecurls. He asked, in Hebrew, where the house of the Ḥakham could be found. At first no one realized that he was speaking Hebrew because of his strange accent. When they finally realized it was Hebrew, they did not understand that it was our Master he was looking for. In the lands from which he came a rabbi is called Ḥakham.

The essence of the matter is that this man had with him a bill of divorce for Zlateh that Aaron had sent. I will not go into details because I want to get to the end of the story. So I pass over the fact that these details contradict what Aaron had explicitly told our Master, namely, that he was dead and had died in such and such a way. Still, the details bear repeating. The man who brought the bill of divorce was a great scholar. In addition to his mastery of Torah in all its aspects, he knew Greek and Arabic. If I remember correctly, our Master, may the memory of the righteous be for a blessing, asked him the meaning of certain terms he had come across in his studies whose meanings were not clear to him. He declared at one point, "If I had the strength, I would compile those words into a lexicon

as an aid to students and especially to those who write halakhic opinions." These last words, "to those who write halakhic opinions," I never
heard directly from our Master but only from reputable people who can
be relied upon never to make statements they have not heard.

The long and the short of it is that the three compartments of Gehinnom that I have noted I saw while completely awake and not in a dream.
The same goes for the judgments visited upon all who talk during the
prayers and the Torah reading. How do we account for the severity of
the punishment? From the following parable that I once heard from our
Master. The time and place when he told it to us are worth noting.

15

On the twentieth of Sivan, about an hour and a half after the morning
service, the whole town went to the cemetery—old men and children,
young men and women, even nursing mothers with their infants. Some
went to visit their relatives' graves, some to entreat the dead to pray for
the living.

That year the local citizenry did not harass us. Even those who had
stolen our houses and then occupied them did not try to humiliate us as
in former years, when they would stand in front of our houses and mock
us with tenderhearted words. "Are you all hungry from the fast? Here,
have some pork. Are you thirsty? Here, have some warm blood. Come,
dear neighbors, take your fill." That year the opposite happened. Many
of them brought out water for us to wash our hands when we left the
cemetery. We washed with that water, and when we got back to town everyone washed again. Some of us suggested that the world was changing
for the better; others conjectured that the Gentiles were leaving us alone
because they were getting tired of murdering us. Then there were others who opined that we Jews had fallen so much that we were no longer
worthy of Esau's efforts to victimize us.

In years past our Master, may the memory of the righteous be for
a blessing, eulogized the victims of the abominable Khmelnitski, may
his name be blotted out, and all others martyred by the Gentiles, in the

cemetery. But when the cemetery was completely filled with graves and people were so crammed together all around that a kohen was once jostled into an area forbidden to kohanim, our Master moved the site of his eulogy to the Great Synagogue and delivered it there after the afternoon service. In his last years, our Master stopped going to the cemetery altogether. He is reported to have said, "Why do I need to go to the dead when they are coming toward me?" What he probably meant was that Buczacz had become one big Jewish cemetery; wherever you started to dig you would find Jewish bodies. He had already begun wondering whether a kohen could even live in Buczacz. I myself never heard him actually say that, but I believe those who say that he did, and I have no reason to doubt them. Whenever our Master was uncertain about a halakhic matter, he did not rest until he clarified it.

When we returned from the cemetery we all went to the Great Synagogue for the afternoon service. As on all public fasts, we read from the Torah the passage beginning *And Moses implored the Lord*, and then the haftarah from the prophets. Our Master, may the memory of the righteous be for a blessing, was called up to recite the haftarah and he chanted it beautifully. When he finished with the words *Thus declares the Lord God who gathers the dispersed of Israel; I will gather still more to those already gathered*, I was quite certain that Isaiah's prophecy was about to be realized, and I had the idea that our Master thought so too.

16

When he had concluded the blessings after the haftarah, our Master picked up the prayer book and chanted the prayer "O Merciful God" for the raising up of the soul of his master, the holy Rabbi Yeḥiel Mikhl of the great town of Nemirov, who was slain for the sanctification of the Divine Name. When he reached the stanza

Precious on earth and in regions supernal,
To us mortal men and to God the eternal;
Proud head from his body the keen sword did sever,
From our shame we beseech you, O Lord us deliver

our Master sobbed in grief, placed the prayer book on the table, and his head slumped down on it. After a while he pulled himself up, and his white earlocks shone like polished silver. The interpreters of mystic secrets said that our Master had bathed his head in the waters of grace. His face shone in the crimson glow of the setting sun, but his eyes were closed, and our Master seemed like one who had been on a distant journey. Those same commentators said that he had returned from the far western edge of the world, where the Divine Presence resides, and there he had seen his master, that holy light Rabbi Mikhl of Nemirov, and all the martyrs with him, sitting in the Academy on High, radiant in the Divine Presence. I do not concern myself with hidden matters—for a person like me what my eyes behold is sufficient—but I agree with those who say that every single one of our Master's curls resembled a silver goblet that has been immersed in pure water. I remember once before Passover they brought him a silver goblet and he looked at it and pronounced it fit to be used as Elijah's cup at the seder. He instructed me to go and immerse it in a mikvah, which I did, and when I took it out the water made it glisten.

There were whispers that our Master was too weak to complete the prayer and they signaled to Reb Ḥizkiah, the prayer leader, to go up and finish. When our Master saw Reb Ḥizkiah coming up, he again took hold of the prayer book and in a heart-rending voice chanted

> Angels unsullied and holy beings pure
> Cry out at the bitterness they must endure;
> How shameful our lot, we are objects of scorn,
> Disgrace and contumely, we are left all forlorn.
> Hellas and Araby together contrive
> That none born of Israel shall live or survive.
> Our God is One and His great name is One,
> Thus may our enemies all be undone.

When our Master said the words "Our God is One and His great name is One," a great dread fell upon him. He placed the prayer book on the table, put his head down upon it, and stood there trembling. A few moments passed until he again picked up the prayer book and chanted

All who are pleasant to behold . . .

when he stopped and handed the prayer book to Reb Ḥizkiah. Reb Ḥizkiah stood there, not knowing if our Master simply wanted to pause and finish the prayer or if he wanted him to complete it. Our Master then with great effort chanted word by word the rest of the prayer as I held in front of him the tablet on which it was inscribed.

When he finished, an argument arose over whether our Master had said "proud head from his body the keen sword did sever" or "proud head from his body the mean sword did sever." In my opinion he said "the keen sword," which is how it was copied on the tablet. It was inappropriate that someone had erased "keen" and written "mean."

After the Aleinu prayer, our Master instructed the aged Reb Meshullam to say the concluding kaddish because he was a descendant of Rabbi Meir ben Isaac, who composed the Akdamut prayer for Shavuot and saved a major Jewish community, and also because he came from Ashkenaz, where there had been much persecution.

After the kaddish our Master instructed Reb Ḥizkiah, the prayer leader, to chant the piyyut "Though few in number we plead before You." Though this poem was composed by Rabbi Meshullam ben Kalonymus for the Fast of Esther, some maintain that our Master intended it to be said on that day so as to remind God that our numbers today are diminished; others hold that he wanted it said because of what had happened to him on Yom Kippur. On Yom Kippur, during the recitation of a piyyut by Meshullam ben Kalonymus, our Master was overcome by weakness and fell asleep, and he wanted to make up for that now on the fast of the twentieth of Sivan with another piyyut by Meshullam. I am inclined to think that he did it for the honor of Rabbi Meshullam ben Kalonymus. The proof is that the next day he sent me to Reb Akiva Shas to borrow the talmudic tractate Zevaḥim, and Reb Akiva asked me if I had ever seen our Master study tractate Gittin. I asked him why he wanted to know that and he told me that the name Kalonymus is mentioned in one of Rashi's comments in tractate Zevaḥim and in a Tosafot note in tractate Gittin. Reb Akiva showed me the place where Rashi writes "This is how the excellent Rabbi Meshullam ben Kalonymus explained it in the hour of his death." He did not point out to me the note in the Tosafot. When I related this matter in the beit midrash, they remarked that it was odd that Reb Akiva forgot to include the note in the Tosafot at the end of tractate Menaḥot in which Rabbi Meshullam is mentioned.

I would mention here in passing that whenever our Master would borrow a volume of the Talmud, he would send as security the Sabbath candelabrum. He had both simple and symbolic reasons for doing this, the simple one being that on Friday when he would be arranging the Sabbath candles he would be reminded to return the Talmud volume, and the symbolic one because Torah is compared to light, and just as a candelabrum supports the light, so the Talmud is the basis on which the Torah rests.

More to the point, I should also note that just before the afternoon service our Master instructed that it be announced that whoever was feeling weak should go home and eat, particularly the sick and women who were pregnant or nursing, all of whom were obligated to break their fast immediately without apology. He had already sent a child who had not yet studied Talmud to go and tell the rabbi's wife to inform Zlateh that he was ordering her to eat and drink. He ordered me to send that same instruction to my wife. Our Master knew exactly when to do this because she was then right at the point of fainting from the fast. It was no wonder that she was fasting. How could a woman who had witnessed the deaths of her father, her mother, her three brothers, and her four sisters, take pleasure from food and drink on that day? But since our Master had commanded her to break her fast, she did eat something. So great was the respect for our Master, may the memory of the righteous be for a blessing, that even tiny babies in their mothers' wombs obeyed him. Tiny babies is an exaggeration, but certainly women and infants.

After that our Master went up to the Holy Ark, with Reb Akiva Shas and Reb Meshullam supporting him on either side. Our Master kissed the curtain in front of the Ark and the doors, and paused for a few moments. Then he began his eulogy for the martyrs of the pogroms of 1648 and 1649, all the righteous and saintly ones who met cruel and gruesome deaths, and all the other men, women, and infants, children of the Holy One, who sanctified His great Name through their deaths. He recited the names of the towns and villages that had been destroyed, and there was not one town or hamlet that he did not mention, and there was not one community of which he did not enumerate the number of Jews killed in it. Some thought that our Master used some biblical verses as a memory aid, but which verses they were was anyone's guess. Some thought they were from the first chapter of the prophet Malachi, but exactly which verses they were was, again, anyone's guess. I always thought they were from the book of Malachi because on the eve of the twentieth of Sivan I found our Master sitting by himself and reciting aloud the verse "*Remember the Torah of My servant Moses . . .*"

17

As the shamash was narrating, the sun glowed crimson from the radiance of the flowers and the red hot stones of Eden, in accordance with the explanation of the reddening of the sun in the late afternoon in the Book of the Angel Razi'el. And so as the sun grew crimson, the time for the afternoon service arrived, and everyone went and washed their hands and recited the passage about the daily sacrificial offering in the Temple and then stood for the silent devotion. The evening service followed immediately. After the Aleinu prayer and the concluding kaddish, they all crowded around the shamash to find out how the matter ended.

The old man looked at them and said, "If you are so intent on listening to stories, how will you be able to hear the sound of the Messiah's shofar on the day when it is sounded? Why do you need to know the end of the story when it was already clear from the beginning? You heard then that we have to be very, very careful not to talk during prayer and certainly not while the Torah is being read." The shamash repeated the word "very" so intensely that everyone began to tremble at the severity of the transgression. After that they stopped asking how the story ended.

But he did not leave it at that and proceeded to tell the story to its end, and his words sank deep into their bones and stayed with them all their days. And when they passed away, they saw in another world everything the shamash had told them in this one.

18

The shamash continued:

Because I treasure every word our Master uttered, I now return to what he said. The details of the story are clear, but the depths of his teachings—who can plumb them, especially now that fifty-four years have passed since they were spoken.

And so our Master stood before the Holy Ark facing the congregation, with Reb Akiva Shas and Reb Meshullam on either side of him. I stood below facing the congregation so as to prevent anyone from pushing forward to go up the bimah, all the while keeping an eye on our Master to be ready at a moment's notice in case he needed me.

Our Master was reaching the end of his eulogy when it looked as if his talit was falling off his left shoulder, as it often did at the end of his sermons and never did when he stood for the silent prayer, when it stayed in place all the time. I heard from Reb Shmuel the scribe that Reb Yosef Halevi, who wrote a book about the victims of the 1648–49 massacres and another about the shofar that the Messiah will one day sound, once opined that our Master's soul belonged to those Rabbi Yoḥanan had in mind when he made the statement in the Talmud, "Would that a person might pray the whole day long." That is why our Master's talit clung to him even after prayer. But this was not the case after his sermons, which in our time have largely become messages of moral instruction and rebuke for the Jewish people's shortcomings. This whole matter can be explained in different ways, and I do not want to belabor it. In any case, it seemed to me that our Master was motioning to me, so I hurried up to him.

He looked at me as if he were puzzled why I was standing next to him. He had definitely motioned me to come up, but since he had taken flight to worlds where people like us can never go, his visage had altered, and what people like us think they see is often not so.

Our Master continued looking at me and quoted the verse that God said to Moses after the sin of the golden calf, *But you remain standing here with Me*. Then he added the verse from the laws in the book of Exodus *By the word of two witnesses or three shall a case be established*. I would be surprised if there was anyone in the synagogue who could fathom our Master's intention. I myself began to understand it only when he was halfway through his sermon, for after he concluded the eulogy he continued to sermonize. That is one thing I take pride in: if I do not understand our Master's words right away, later on I do. I heard from the saintly Rabbi Isaac the Chastiser, the son of Reb Yedidiah Lieberman, the nephew of the holy Rabbi Mikhl of Nemirov, may the Lord avenge his blood, that the deeds of the righteous correspond to their thoughts, and therefore their words are coherent from beginning to end.

19

Our Master began as follows: "My brothers, dear members of the congregation, you who love God, blessed be His holy name. I will offer no words of rebuke today, for God has visited upon us a double measure of punishment for our transgressions." Our Master turned to the Holy Ark and said: "You, O Lord, know that I had in mind only the sins known to us. Our hidden sins and iniquities and transgressions are known only to You." He then recited a verse from the book of Ezra. Which one it was I forget because I could not find a single copy of the full Bible anywhere in town and thus was unable to check the text. Our Master then turned to the congregation and continued: "God is righteous, and so our only task is to ask for the strength to withstand our sufferings until He will deem them sufficient. And we must never stop hoping for them to end"—and here our Master wiped away a tear with his talit. That tear was surprising, for our Master never teared up in public except when he mentioned his holy teacher, may God redeem his blood. When he faced God in prayer he certainly shed tears, but not when he faced people. This is why I think his eyes always glistened and a light shone from them, even in the hour of his passing.

Our Master continued: "Nor will I offer any words of Torah. Words of Torah require a joyful heart and a clear mind, and all of us here today are weighed down by mourning and fasting. But the day is long and we stand in a holy place sanctified by Torah and prayer, and so let us say some things about Torah and prayer. In truth, in a holy place we should not even speak about mundane matters, but since I want to talk about silence, let speech come and serve the cause of silence."

Here our Master stopped talking and just stood there. I stood beside him in mute astonishment and the whole congregation stood in hushed silence. Nothing stirred in the synagogue other than the rustle of his snowy white curls. Because of headaches resulting from an old sword wound, our Master never shaved his head, even for Shavuot. Then he raised his eyes and looked out upon the assembled. He scrutinized each and every person to see how much he could absorb.

After surveying the congregation, our Master closed his eyes and said: "Though I have not seen it, I have heard that there are people who do not restrain themselves from talking during the services and even while the Torah is being read. I am not referring to those who are compelled by circumstances to do so. Rather, I have in mind those whose vocal chords function independently, everywhere, all the time, on any subject, for no purpose in particular and for no purpose in general, even during the services, even during the reading of the Torah. When you tell such people that what they are doing is not appropriate, they answer you by saying that, yes, it is indeed forbidden to talk during the services, and so on. Do you think they hear what they are saying? No, they continue chattering away. Then there are those who, when you rebuke them for talking, reply, 'For only two or three words spoken aloud you are making such a fuss?'

"And so, my beloved friends, as I have said, I am not here to chastise you for the sin of talking during the services and the Torah reading.

One only rebukes those whose actions demand it, whereas you have been blessed by God not to be guilty of this transgression, and you are not in need of my reprimand. But since we are in a house of God consecrated to Torah and prayer, and since it is customary to offer admonitions concerning this particular sin, let me say a few words about it. Not by castigating you but by way of a parable.

"The midrash on Song of Songs states that a parable should not be regarded as something trivial. It can lead us to understand what the Torah is saying. The midrash offers a parable itself to illustrate this point. A king had a gold coin or a precious pearl that went missing in his palace. How would he find it? With a pennyworth wick of the candle that would lead him to it. Likewise, a parable can lead us to discover what the Torah is saying. So do not regard it as a trivial thing."

The shamash interrupted his narration and observed:
Most people today know this parable, but in our Master's day collections of midrash were largely unavailable, except for Midrash Tanhuma, and so any teaching from the midrash was regarded as something brand new. Furthermore, whenever our Master would cite a parable from the Talmud or the midrash, he quoted it word for word, as "it is like a king who. . . ." But when he told a parable in his own words he never introduced it that way. I once heard a theory about this. In the past, kings had stature and were worthy examples for parables; today, when their power has been diminished, as is the case with the Polish kings who did not rise up to save themselves during the Khmelnitski pogroms, it is not flattering to compare anything to them. I now return to the words of our Master, may the memory of the righteous be for a blessing.

20

"I bring the parable I will tell not to illuminate a point in the Torah but to illuminate a point about transgression against it. Maimonides, of blessed memory, says in his Code that it is a positive commandment to pray each day, as it is written, *You shall serve the Lord your God.* The Oral

Tradition teaches that 'serving' entails prayer, as it is written, *And serve Him with all your heart*, and the Sages have taught, What is the service of the heart? It is prayer."

Whenever he quoted a biblical verse our Master would recite it in a melody, the way a melamed teaches Torah to children, and he would explain it as he went along. Each one would receive it according to his capacity. There were about two hundred householders in Buczacz in our Master's day, besides servants and wayfarers, and they all eagerly drank in his words.

Our Master then noted that according to the opinion of Nahmanides the commandment to pray is rabbinically ordained, and then he cited Maimonides' view in his Book of the Commandments that prayer is a commandment mandated by the Torah itself. He analyzed both positions and came out for Maimonides' view and against that of Nahmanides, after which he turned to Reb Akiva Shas and asked him, "Is this not so, Reb Akiva?" Reb Akiva nodded and said, "Certainly, certainly." Flustered, he added, "But does our Master need me to agree?" The interpreters of mystic secrets explained his seeking Reb Akiva's opinion this way: according to those who delve into secret wisdom, Nahmanides was descended from the right earlock of the great teacher Rabbi Akiva, and since our Master was going against Nahmanides' view, he sought confirmation for his approach from Reb Akiva Shas in deference to Reb Akiva's venerable namesake. Personally, I have no concern with secret matters. Would that I could comprehend even a fraction of the Torah's revealed meaning.

Our Master then began to explain the sublimity of prayer, which enables a mortal human being, born of woman, fashioned from the dust, and food for the worms, to extol the eternal living and exalted holy God, and even to beseech Him for our needs. Then he dwelt on the sublimity of the Hebrew language, from which our prayers are formed, and on the secret of the holy tongue, which holds the mystery of the perfect unity, and which was bestowed before the sin in the Garden of Eden and certainly before human speech was confounded and diffused into seventy tongues. Our Master expressed it in these words: "Come and see how great prayer is. In prayer a person can raise himself up to the original state he was in before the generation of the tower of Babel; for at that time, as we find in the book Gates of Light, God apportioned the nations among the angels on high and reserved Israel for Himself, since Israel is an element of the supernal God." Here our Master looked out at the entire congregation, householders and craftsmen, servants and wayfarers, surveying them all in a single glance. He pulled his talit over his forehead, causing the phylactery on his head to jut out under it and create an opening on the side through which his white curls fell out. They were illumined by all the shining lights, light from above and light from below, the light of the setting sun and the light of the memorial candles burning as on Yom Kippur. There was not a man or women who did not light a candle in memory of their departed. Even beggars and those who could only afford to light them on Sabbath eve and holidays, even those who were wards of charity—they all borrowed candles to light.

As our Master stood there between the Ark and the congregation, he added, "In the Midrash ha-ne'elam we find that the idea of creating Israel arose in the divine mind before the creation of the world and even before the creation of the angels. Because of God's great love for them they were destined to be called Israel, which is God's name. In the Pirke de Rabbi Eliezer it is told that when Jacob asked the angel 'What is your name?' the angel bestowed upon him his own name, Israel." Our Master again looked around at all the people in the synagogue, householders and craftsmen, servants and wayfarers, and then said in his sweet-sounding voice, "Israel! An element of the supernal God! An element of the supernal God!" I do not remember if he actually repeated that phrase or if I just think he did. As the saying in the Talmud goes, "the nobleman took hold of me and his fragrance rubbed off on my hand." Because I served our Master, his voice resounds within me. These are profound and sublime matters, and not every mind can handle them.

21

Our Master picked up his talit with both hands, one on each side, laid it back on his neck, and paused for a moment. No one could tell whether he had concluded his sermon or if he had more to add, but we were all quite prepared to continue standing and listening, even those who were weak from the fast. The synagogue then did not yet have benches to sit on, other than a chair for the rabbi and one for Elijah the prophet.

The heart knows its own bitterness. We knew in our heart that this was our Master's last sermon, may the memory of the righteous be for a blessing. On Hoshana Rabba, when we got to the prayer "Answer the faithful," his voice lost its resonance, and on the day after Simḥat Torah he passed into eternal life. I do not want to interrupt what I am relating here but I would only note that the reward of humility is grace, and our Master's humility in life was matched only by his grace in death.

And so all of us remained standing, waiting to hear more. Even the little boys who could not stand still even for a minute stood motionless. Whether they understood what was being said or not is uncertain, but words of truth are always eagerly heard even if they are not understood.

Our Master loosened his talit from around his neck, lifted his hands in gratitude, and the light in his eyes took in the entire congregation. In his pleasant voice he said, "The three Patriarchs did us a great kindness when they instituted the prayer services, and after them, the men of the Great Assembly when they arranged the order of the prayers, and, no less importantly, the reading of the Torah, which was ordained by Moses to be read on Sabbaths, festivals, New Moons, and the intermediate days of the festivals, as it is written *And Moses announced the festivals of the Lord to the children of Israel.* Ezra ordained that Israel should read from the Torah on Mondays, Thursdays, and at the afternoon service on the Sabbath." For each of these points our Master cited their sources in the Babylonian Talmud, the Jerusalem Talmud, the midrashic collections Sifre, Sifra, and Mekhilta, the Tosafot, Alfasi, Rambam, and the Tur—all these sources he cited by heart. Most of them he had not seen since the day he left Nemirov, where he studied with his holy teacher, may the Lord redeem his blood. I have heard that the faculty of memory is a male attribute and the faculty of forgetting a female one, as is implied in the verse *Hearken, O daughter, take note and incline your ear, forget your people and your father's house.* We see there that forgetfulness goes with being a daughter. Today there are individuals in Buczacz who own more holy books than there were in the entire town in our Master's day. I know of a great scholar, the rabbi of several communities, who at the time of his passing remarked that while it is certainly hard to take leave of a world in which one can acquire the merits of Torah, commandments, and good deeds, in the Academy on High he would get to see tractate 'Eruvin, which he never laid eyes on in his lifetime. I also remember two yeshiva students who once came to our town after walking for two days, so they could view the minor tractates, having heard that there was here in Buczacz a man who owned all the volumes of the Talmud.

Let us return to our Master's sermon. After he explained the commandment of the public reading of the Torah, he raised his talit above his shoulders, covered his head, and said, "The Holy One, blessed be He, has done us a great kindness, for when a person sits in the synagogue he hears the words of the Torah that God gave to Israel." Again he lowered his talit onto his shoulders, placed both his arms on the podium in front of him, rested his head upon them, and told of certain elders, of whom it was said by those who know of such matters, that during the reading of the Torah they ascended to the spiritual level Israel was at when the Torah was given.

Our Master further related the following: "When I was studying in the yeshiva of my great teacher, luminary of the ages, there came to town a preacher who asked my Master's permission to speak in the Great Synagogue on the Sabbath. The weekly Torah portion was Yitro, and when my Master asked him what he would talk about, the preacher replied that his subject would be the Ten Commandments. When my Master asked him to be more specific, the preacher replied that the Ten Commandments in this Torah portion are meant for this world and the Ten Commandments in Deuteronomy for the world to come. To which my Master said, 'I do not know this world and I do not know the next one;

all I know is what is put forth in the verse *Would that they had this heart of theirs to fear Me and keep My commands for all time so that it would go well with them and with their children forever'."*

Our Master, may the memory of the righteous be for a blessing, melodiously repeated the entire verse, and when he intoned the words *so that it would go well with them and with their children forever,* everyone knew that to fear God and to obey His commandments *was* what it meant for it to go well with us and our children forever.

22

Our Master continued: "Now that we have seen the grandeur of prayer and the sanctity of the Torah, let me say something about the conversations people conduct while the congregation is praying and reading from the Torah.

"Reb Zevulun the spice merchant, may he rest in peace, told me that he once heard from some far-roaming travelers about a desert that lies beyond the land of Cush. In that desert there is a certain species of monkeys that look like dogs and whose main food is ants. When one of these monkeys goes out hunting and notices an anthill, it places one of its paws over the anthill, buries itself in the sand so as to make itself invisible, and pretends to be asleep. The ants in turn see what they think is a nice soft hill in which to live, and they leave their dens in which they have stored their food. Whole armies of them crawl out and climb up the hill without knowing that an animal's paw lies underneath. The remaining ants see this and are also drawn to the hill, and they all crawl all over the monkey's paw, completely unaware that they stand on the very site of their destruction and that a dangerous animal lies in wait to devour them. The monkey lies there covered in sand, its paw covering the ants, the entire colony of which has by now left its den and been drawn to this hill. When the paw is completely full of ants, the monkey opens its mouth and swallows then all with one gulp.

"Like life in that desert, so is our existence in this world, and like that monkey who looks like a dog, so is Satan who bedevils Israel. And we, the remnant of Israel, the house of Jacob—how tiny are we, O Israel, how feeble our strength—we are like ants, of which Scripture says, *They are a people without power, yet they prepare food for themselves in summer*, and of which it is further written *Go to the ant, you sluggard, study its ways and learn*. And yet with all its wisdom, the ant cannot avoid falling into the hands of the monkey.

"Dearly beloved brothers, perhaps I see this matter so clearly that I have not explained it to you adequately, so let me say it another way. It is well known that Israel's house of prayer is called a nest, as we learn from the psalm, *How lovely is Your dwelling place, O Lord of hosts, I long, I yearn for the courts of the Lord, my body and soul shout for joy to the living God*, after which the psalmist continues, *Even the sparrow has found a home, and the swallow a nest for herself in which to set her young near Your altar, O Lord of hosts, my king and my God. Happy are they who dwell in Your house. . . .* Now we can understand what Job meant when he said *I will die with my nest*: if I will not merit to fulfill the psalmist's prayer *and I shall dwell in the house of the Lord all the days of my life*, then I hope that when I die, I die there, my soul expiring in prayer to the living God."

The memorial candles burned brightly as candles do when it gets dark. Our Master looked at them and said, "The sun is about to set, the day is nearly done, so I will be brief and speak only to the point here. I would only cite Rabbi Ibn Ezra on the verse I have just noted, *and the swallow a nest for herself in which to set her young near Your altar, O Lord of hosts*. Ibn Ezra quotes a commentator who explains that there is a certain kind of bird that flies away from settled areas where people live and makes its nest near the special place where sacrifices are offered to the blessed God, so that it might merit seeing its young near the altar. Now we know that no birds nested in the Holy Temple, as the Radak pointed out, and even Ibn Ezra himself disagreed with what that commentator wrote. In any case, his reference provides a fitting metaphor for Israel, who, like that bird, sets its *young near Your altar, O Lord of hosts, my king and my God*.

"One more thing before I return to the matter at hand. It is well known that the abode of the Messiah is called a bird's nest. It is less well known that this nest rests upon the prayers that Israel offers. How careful, then, must one be not to talk while the congregation is praying so as not, God forbid, to topple the nest from its perch.

"The press of time and the many facets of the matter have kept me from interpreting all the lessons of the parable. Nevertheless, we can see the parallel between the monkey in the parable and Satan in its lesson. Monkey and Satan both want the same thing: to fill their bellies, the former by stretching forth its paw and ensnaring ants, the latter by sticking out his hand to grab the words of Israel's prayers and of the Torah and stuff his belly with them.

"*Praised be the Name of the Lord who hears the prayers of His people Israel. He will not reject those who have been banished.* There is not a prayer or a single word of Torah that goes to the wrong place. Still, a person should be very mindful about talking or conversing during the service and the Torah reading so that his prayers not go to a place where we do not want them to go."

Our Master took the corners of his talit, one in each hand, and tucked them into his sash. Or maybe it was just his hands he tucked in and not the corners of his talit—I do not recall. In any case, when he was praying, his tzitzit swung around freely. I mention this because I have seen a new practice that our ancestors never imagined, that of tucking the corners of the talit into the sash the way laborers on the job fold the hem of their shirt under their belt.

23

Our Master added, "Our days are as a passing shadow, but each day itself is long and drawn out, so let us temper our remaining time of mourning and fasting with another parable.

"It is common wisdom that there is no person who does not suffer, and who knows this better than the people of Israel? My parable is about such a person. There was a person to whom trouble befell, and he was unable to deliver himself from it. He looked all over for help. He heard that very near him, not far away, there lived a lord in a castle, a ruler who was as powerful as he was righteous and as righteous as he was caring. The man rose early and went to see him. When the lord of the castle saw this Jew walking about in the courtyard, he commanded that the man be brought to him. The man went in and began to tell the lord of his trouble. The lord of the castle was filled with compassion for him. Remember that this lord of the castle had many means at his disposal, and when he took pity on a person he had the ability to help him. As the Jew stood and recounted his heartaches, he began to digress about other things and brought up all sorts of irrelevant matters. Talk of one thing led to talk of another and very soon the man was uttering the most frivolous things that in any other place would not even be worth mentioning, all the more so before the lord of the castle. Whereupon the lord of the castle said to himself, Why need I bother with his trifles? If he is looking for trivial things, what is he doing here? There is verse that confirms him in this judgment, as it is written, *Who has asked this of you, that you come and trample My courts.*

"So now consider that the lord of the castle is the Master of all worlds who has the power to help us and deliver us at all times. When a Jew comes before Him to beseech Him for help and to plead for his life, is it not perfectly obvious and self-evident that when he opens his mouth he should be careful not to utter anything unnecessary and not to burden God, so to speak, with having to listen to things that are inappropriate and irrelevant? *The Lord is near to all who call upon Him, to all who call upon him in truth*, and not to those who talk of empty things and engage in idle conversations.

"This in regard to prayer. Now let me say something about the Torah reading. There was a certain poor man to whom the lord of the castle took a liking. He extended to him the kindness of letting him settle on his land, confirming his consent in writing so as to prevent anyone from seizing what had been granted to him or cheating him out of it. The lord then read to the poor man the document of attestation so that he would know what was his. One would assume that the poor man would listen, since his whole right to live and dwell on the land depended on that document. The poor man not only did not listen, he interrupted the lord in his reading, thus showing contempt for the one who sought to do him good and harming himself by not paying attention to what was being given to him.

"My friends and dearly beloved brothers, the Holy One, blessed be He, has shown us a special love and extended to us the kindness of giving us the Torah, which is the document that attests to Israel's existence and to the right we have merited to live in this world, our right to be here at all. So when we open the Torah and read it in public, we should sit in fear and awe, in dignity and in joy in knowing what God has given us. But what do we do? We interrupt His words and chatter away. We not only are heedless of what God has given us, we are also, heaven forbid, showing contempt for the living God.

"Where there is too much talk, blame will not be lacking. All of us here are afflicted, downtrodden, and hurting, no part of us has not been ravaged, and so I will put an end to words. We who are Israel, the people of God, who trust in the shelter of our Creator, let us gather strength for the honor of the synagogue, which serves us in place of the Holy Temple, and let us pay attention to our prayers, which are our conversation with God, and listen to the words of our Torah, God's conversation with us, the people of Israel. May the One who in mercy and in favor hears the prayer uttered by every single person of Israel, receive in mercy all our prayers. And may we merit fulfilling all the words of the Torah. Amen. May thus be His will."

After kissing the Ark curtain, our Master turned toward the congregation and his face showed great sadness. I have heard two reasons for this. One is that he grew sad after every sermon, because, being a great preacher, he was worried that the beauty of his words overshadowed the message he was imparting. The other is that he worried lest he had said something that was not for the sake of Heaven. Years later, after I had remarried, and Zlateh, may she rest in peace, was my wife, I heard from her that after every sermon he delivered, our Master took upon himself a full-day fast of silence.

Since I have mentioned the matter of abstaining from speech, I shall relate something I heard from the leader of the service, Reb Ḥizkiah. Reb Ḥizkiah's forebears came from Aleppo and before that from Babylonia. Circumstances required them to wander through many lands until one day they came to Poland. Reb Ḥizkiah heard from his elders that there were in the lands where they wandered great sages who took upon themselves a full-day fast of silence not only during the Ten Days of Penitence, as do some Jews here in the Kingdom of Poland, but who were silent almost all the time. No worldly or mundane word came out of their mouths. In their eagerness to assist those sages, people tried to learn their different gestures so they could fathom their wishes. But the desire for things of this world is rooted in the power of speech, and the sages eventually lost all such desire. There is a verse in the book of Proverbs that hints at this, but Reb Ḥizkiah never told it to me. I think the one he had in mind is in chapter 30.

The shamash further related another story in the name of Reb Ḥizkiah: There was a porter in Aleppo named Benjamin who never uttered one unnecessary word even if it involved his work. This Benjamin's face glowed with a light that was not seen even on the faces of great scholars, and when he died the one who eulogized him quoted the verse in Moses' final blessing, *Of Benjamin he said, Beloved of the Lord, he rests securely beside Him; ever does He protect him, as he rests between His shoulders.* The local rabbi heard about this and became angry. In a dream he heard declaimed to him the verse in Jacob's final blessing *Benjamin is a ravenous wolf* and he understood that his life was in danger. He rose early, gathered ten men, and went and prostrated himself on the porter's grave and begged his forgiveness.

24

The shamash's words left Buczacz astounded. Talking generally brings people together and dispels worry, while silence is usually a sign of sorrow and suffering, as we see in the verse *Let him sit alone and keep silent.* But now each one began to spout his own personal interpretation of what had been said, and they very nearly forgot the incident that touched off the whole story. The story itself they knew, but its import they forgot.

This dispirited the shamash. All those years he had kept his mouth shut, and now by opening it, he gave them an opening to fabricate all kinds of things. He looked up at them sternly, but they paid him no attention and continued talking. Until he interrupted their prattle, saying, "Now that you have heard what you have heard, I do not need to remind you that I did what I did not out of disrespect but out of pity on a fellow Jew, and I took upon myself the sin of embarrassing him in public. So now consider my case and judge me as you will. For my part, I affirm the integrity of my judges and accept whatever verdict they render."

That brought them back to ponder the original issue before them and that they still faced, namely if they would pray with concentrated intention, the Holy One, blessed be He, would receive their prayers in mercy and favor. Likewise, if they would properly direct their hearts during the reading of the Torah, they could reach the level that Israel attained when the Torah was given at Mt. Sinai. But we, what do we do? The mouths that we were given to utter God's praise speak trivialities, and the ears through which we were to hear the words of Torah we abandon to banalities.

A series of groans came forth from the assembled. First from despair, then from trepidation, for even when one takes care not to talk during the services or the Torah reading, there are times when one simply cannot control oneself and things that serve purposes neither lofty nor base come out. Or sometimes a quip suggests itself, as for instance when the cantor sings the wrong melody, or the Torah reader uses the wrong cantillation, or mispronounces the vowels. And sometimes an affected piety takes hold of the congregation and they make the Torah reader repeat phrases unnecessarily, and then they all start quibbling over just why he had to go back. The result is a failure to hear not just the word in question but also the words before and after it. Jewish law is clear that if a complete weekly Torah portion is not read in public on its scheduled Sabbath, it must be read on the following Sabbath together with the portion slated for that week, for when we miss out on Torah, we are always given a chance to make up the loss. Therefore we are by law obligated to be careful not to lose out on any Torah reading. Yet because of our many sins not a Sabbath goes by when we do not miss hearing some words of the Torah because of idle chatter and needless conversations.

25

After that moment of truth, many woke up to the fact that talking during the services, not to mention during the reading of the Torah, is indeed a serious offense. Just how serious they were only now beginning to comprehend. They took it upon themselves to be careful not to talk not only during the services but even from the moment they entered the synagogue until the time they left. And so they did. A few began to be mindful to say nothing unnecessary even at home and in the marketplace, for nothing is more harmful to a person than needless words. A person says things that are uncalled for and eventually has to deny that he said them, which means he has to lie. Why does he lie? Because he spoke words that were not called for. But our main concern here is Torah and prayer, so let us return to the shamash and his story.

Everyone crowded around the shamash and badgered him with questions, some intelligent, some foolish. For example, if the population of Gehinnom increases, will the distance between one person and another decrease? Or, "Since you visited Gehinnom on the day after Yom Kippur, and the repentance undertaken on that day influences worlds beyond this one, did you notice any purifying effect on the wicked in Gehinnom?" Still another question was, "Did you see any angels among the inhabitants of Gehinnom, since it is written *His angels He charges with folly*, and we know that there is no favoritism before God, and so if angels go astray, do they go to Gehinnom? And if they do, do they go with their wings on? And are their wings affected by the fire of Gehinnom?" There was no end to their questions, and because they had not yet learned to restrain their tongues, those tongues nattered on with abandon.

There were other questions, too: Where do the praises that Gehinnom utters in Perek Shira belong? Some prayer books place them after the ones uttered by all the different creatures, while our prayer books put them with the verses sung by heaven, earth, and the Garden of Eden. Furthermore, if the din of Gehinnom reverberates from one end of the world to the other, which is louder, the praises Gehinnom sings or that din? And what about Sabbath in Gehinnom? We know that the wicked there rest on that day, but does Gehinnom itself fall silent for the day, and do the praises it sings stop? And when it utters its praises, what pronunciation does Gehinnom use? Are certain vowels pronounced the way those newly arrived there pronounce them, as the mystical tradition has it? Others wondered, If wicked people in Gehinnom are judged for twelve months, and we have learned that after twelve months the body ceases to exist and the soul rises up into the next world and does not descend again, then are the wicked still standing there as they were, with their clothes and prayer shawls on? Are scholars impervious to the fiery glow of Gehinnom? There was no end to their questions and theories, for they had not yet learned to restrain their tongues, and so they talked on and on.

The shamash did not answer all the questions put to him, nor did he tell all that he had seen. Not everything needs to be told, and what is told does not always need be spelled out in detail, unless doing so serves some purpose such as bringing people to repentance. The punishment for a sin of this kind must be spelled out, but not necessarily for others. The sages have already told us what is good and what God requires of us, and we, the people of Israel, do try to fulfill what our Creator desires. But in every generation something arises that weakens our ability to perform the commandments, especially a commandment that is necessary for that particular generation. Had God not opened our eyes to this, we would never have survived. Sometimes He makes it known through an event, and sometimes He only gives us a hint; sometimes it is obvious and sometimes we have to figure it out. The illustrious and excellent Rabbi Moshe went to Gehinnom for the sole purpose of freeing his young relative from the chains of her agunah status, and he took the shamash along with him only to light the way with his lantern. Yet in the end the warrant for her release came from elsewhere, and as for the shamash, he told us what he found, including the punishment those who commit this sin receive after they die. Let not this account of sin and punishment become simply a story, a story that one hears for the sheer pleasure of it. Such pleasure has been the downfall of many. But there are many kinds of pleasure, and happy is the one whose pleasure brings him edification and whose edification is his pleasure.

26

Thus did Buczacz come to understand what we see every day: a man does something good for his fellow and nevertheless is punished. Here was an old man who saved a Jew from Gehinnom and they tried to deprive him of his livelihood and dismiss him from his position. By describing the punishment for a transgression that, because of the proliferation of our sins, has tripped up many, including scholars who are supposed to be exemplars, the shamash did a service for many more people than the one he tried to help. The fact is that there are many in this world who appear to be righteous, but in the next one, where truth reigns, they are accounted as absolute sinners, as the shamash saw that night he visited Gehinnom. But now let us take leave of such spurious tsadikim and return to our story.

Buczacz made amends with the shamash. Some did it with words and some with deeds. The first to reconcile with him was, appropriately, the leading light of the community, the father-in-law of the man the shamash had thrown out of the beit midrash for talking during the Torah reading. It is a tribute to the wealthy men of Buczacz that their money does not blind them to the truth and does not fool them into thinking that because they are rich they can dictate what the truth is or what they want it to be. On the contrary, they accept the truth no matter what its source and acknowledge it as the supreme attribute, the virtue personified by the patriarch Jacob, as it is written, *You will ascribe truth to Jacob*. The magnate made amends with the shamash with more than words; he sent him a flask of raisin wine sufficient for kiddush and havdalah for several Sabbaths. And as with the father-in-law, so, too, did the son-in-law, with anguish and deep remorse, beg forgiveness from the shamash for the embarrassment the beit din had caused him. Then in turn came the pious men and the rest of the congregation. Some wanted to forget the angry words they had spoken about dismissing him from his position; some said they really hadn't said what they said; some belittled the whole act of talking, some praised the virtue of silence. Since they had not yet learned to curtail their words, they waxed verbose both in praise of silence and in belittlement of speech.

If I were to report everything that was said, there would be no end here. But there is one thing I will note, namely, that all the days of the week are equal in the opportunities they offer for sinning through speech. Monday, Thursday, and Sabbath are not superior in that respect to Sunday, Tuesday, Wednesday, and Friday, even if the Torah is read on the former three days (corresponding to the three patriarchs) and is not read on the latter four (corresponding to the four matriarchs, as women are exempt from the commandment to study Torah). Therefore, if some Torah idea or nice interpretation or some brilliant new hidush or explanation or explication occurs to you while you are standing before your Maker or are hearing the Torah being read—suppress them and let them not be heard. King Solomon, may he rest in peace, the wisest of all men, took many foreign wives because he knew that there were present in each of them sparks of purity, and he hoped, by marrying them, to tame sin and eradicate transgression. In the end they led him astray. Similarly, during the service or the Torah reading, a person wants to share with his friend a nice thought that came to him, and look what happens to him. May we not end up like him.

27

No one left the communal meeting chamber without committing themselves not to talk during the service from the moment the leader would begin with the prayer "Blessed be the One who spoke" until after the Aleinu prayer, and certainly not during the Torah reading. Some went so far as to commit themselves to remain silent even during the pauses in the Torah reading after each aliyah, when the blessings on behalf of each individual called up to the Torah are customarily made. Doing that would entail a loss of income for the synagogue, but the rabbis concluded that the gains from such silences would outweigh the losses. Consider, for example, what would be going through the mind of someone called up to the Torah: instead of paying attention to the words on the scroll being read as he stood there, he would be trying to figure out exactly who he would designate to be named in the subsequent blessing, and calculating how much he would pledge on that person's behalf. Whether the person he named was worthy of the blessing or if he somehow got misled into designating a person he had no intention of having blessed, the fact is that he would be giving priority to names like Getzel or Feivel or Feivush, Koppel, Berel, and Shmerl over the holy names in the Torah, where each and every word is holy. Moreover, sometimes he could get the names mixed up, and the person who was blessed was not the one he wanted blessed, and the person he wanted blessed was not. Then the one who was blessed unintentionally would think that for twelve pence pledged on his behalf the donor was currying favor with him, and he would come to despise him, as he despised all flatterers, while the one who was supposed to be blessed and was not would secretly regard the donor as an ingrate, a man who, when he asks you to do him a favor and you do it, then goes and blesses everyone in the world but the one he should. What is the cause of all such rancor and resentment and jealousy? The interrupting of the Torah reading for these blessings. But then, how could the synagogue afford to lose the money pledged for those blessings? The solution would be to have all pledges made at the very end, after the reading of the haftarah. That way no money would be mentioned in the presence of the Torah scroll, for even if the money pledged was kosher, the names for the currency were not. They were either named for some unsavory king or they had idolatrous overtones.

I spoke before of twelve pence. In the past a penny was worth much more than it is now, and people donated twelve pence to correspond to the twelve tribes of Israel. Poor people gave three for the three patriarchs or two for the two tablets of the Ten Commandments. Today, however, when it takes one hundred pence to buy what you could once get for a penny, people donate eighteen or twenty-six pence or more, according to whatever gematria calculation occurs to them.

But let me get back to how things unfolded. The assembly did not break up until it was determined that henceforth the shamash would stand on the bimah throughout the entire service, from beginning to end, and if he would see anyone talking he would rap on the table top regardless of whether the offender was an important member of the community, or a rich man, or the son-in-law of a rich man, a scholar, a ruffian, or someone who had privileges at the court. Normally in the Great Synagogue a rap on the table top could not be heard because of the crowd, but now the shamash would bang on the Pralnik book as he might during the repetition of the silent devotion to signal the congregation to respond Amen, or as he might when he was about to make an announcement. And what, you may ask, is the Pralnik book? A bunch of empty pages bound together like a book on which you bang a stick the way a woman beats her laundry to get the water out. The congregation further ordained that the cantor include a special blessing on behalf of all who take care not to utter a word in the synagogue from the time the leader of the service begins the prayer "Blessed be the One who spoke" until the service is concluded. This special blessing was instituted in Buczacz by our forbears on the very first Sabbath after they arrived there, before they founded the actual town of Buczacz, as I have told elsewhere. They brought the blessing with them from the Rhineland, where local custom went back to the days of such renowned rabbis as Rabbenu Gershom, Light of the Exile, Rabbi Shimon the Great, the eminent Rabbi Meshullam ben Kalonymus, and the other illustrious sages of Ashkenaz, may they rest in peace, whose traditions were authoritative in Buczacz in former days.

In order tc end authority to these new directives it was instructed that they be inscribed in the pinqas, the great communal register, because anything written down there was meticulously followed. They further instructed that the entire story told by the shamash also be recorded in the pinqas, because stories awaken the heart, especially of those who cannot picture something unless they read it in writing. So shortly thereafter a scribe wrote out all the details of the story, and he considered it so important that he decided to begin it on a new page in the pinqas lest it get lost among all the things written there previously. The town leaders then read the story and decided that it deserved a wider hearing beyond Buczacz. They agreed amongst themselves that should anyone ever find himself in another town, he would be sure to tell there the whole tale, certainly if he would see someone talking during the service or the reading of the Torah. And he would tell it without fear of intimidation by any of the locals, for the impudent pass on while the word of our God stands firm forever.

So the scribe wrote out the whole story in words true and wise, in the way words were used in Buczacz at the time when Buczacz was Buczacz. Some of the words were from the Torah, some from the sages, all of them had an eloquence that gives tongue to knowledge. The town leaders read the document and showed it to the local maskilim. In Buczacz and the Kingdom of Poland of those days, the term maskilim referred to men broadly learned in many branches of wisdom, men who exemplified the ideal of *Understanding and knowing Me*. It did not apply to those who strayed from the path of reason, of whom David complained, *Is there any man of understanding who seeks after God?* The maskilim read what was written and saw that the scribe indeed had a sophisticated sense of style and grammar, and they acknowledged it, one with words of praise, one with a simple nod of the head. There was one who equivocated and could not say whether it was good or bad, for it is human nature that what one person deems beautiful, another does not. In the end, though, even he admitted that the scribe had expressed everything exactly as it was meant to be written.

The scribe took the document and looked it over a few times, changing a word here, a phrase there. Sometimes the revisions needed are apparent to a writer from the language itself, and sometimes simply from how the words look to him on the page. The writer has to struggle might-ily until he finds the appropriate words, and then when he thinks he has found them, others occur to him that look even better. Were it not for the mercies of Heaven, this process of revision could go on forever. Only a writer who is a fool will think that he has found exactly the right words; a wise one knows that the only correct words are the ones revealed in the Torah, the prophets, and the other books of the Bible. Therefore, the more a writer truly knows the Hebrew language, the more anxious he will be that in his writing he may have, Heaven forfend, tarnished a word.

Why is it that all the other languages are spoken and written without difficulty, whereas Hebrew requires that every word be given extra consideration and that careful attention be paid to word order and syntax? Because all the other languages were devised by humans, whereas Hebrew is the language in which the Torah was given and with whose letters the world was created. Just as there is no letter in the Torah that does not hold great significance, so there is nothing in the world that is superfluous, because everything is ordered as God desires. In the same way, anything composed in Hebrew, the language of holiness, cannot have words that are superfluous or anything in it that is out of place. Hebrew is special for other reasons too, as those who have studied the matter know.

After he made his corrections, the scribe sat down and copied everything out in a handsome script, the letters written the way they were written in Buczacz at the time when Buczacz was Buczacz, each letter distinct unto itself and each one in its place on the line, like people standing for the silent devotion, where the tall ones stick up like a *lamed* and the short ones are small as a *yod*, and all of them are directed to the same place. Had the pinqas not been consumed in the flames, we could have read the entire story just as it was set down in its true and original form, with the unique blend of wisdom and faith that marked all that our ancestors wrote and did and thought and said. But now that book is no more, and Buczacz is destroyed, and many thousands of Jews have been slain, the least of them the equal of the most eminent of the Gentiles, who watched the loathsome monsters destroy the world and did nothing. From our town there were those who were buried alive in graves they dug for themselves; there were those who were never buried; and there were those upon whom the murderers poured kerosene and were immolated one by one, limb by limb.

So now, since that pinqas went up in the flames, and Buczacz has been destroyed, and the deeds of the former generations have been forgotten in the recent suffering, I pondered the possibility that the Gehinnom of our time would make us forget the Gehinnom that the shamash saw, and the story about it, and all we can learn from that story. So I said to myself, Let me put it all down in a book and thus create a memorial to a holy community that sanctified its life in its death as its ancestors sanctified their lives with Torah, which is our life.

(And may I achieve some merit if what I write will motivate some denizens of Jerusalem. For I have seen even here in Jerusalem, the holy city, the gate of heaven, from whence all prayers ascend, that there are people who sit in synagogues and houses of study and talk during the service and the reading of the Torah. I asked my pen, Will you join me in writing this story? And my pen said, Give me your words and I will put your story down on paper. I gave it my words and now the story is written on paper.

Would that my toil has not been for naught nor my effort in vain. And that all who guard their mouth and their tongue will give honor to their Maker and sit in fear and in awe before the One who is above all praise, when the Torah is being read and the prayers are being said, on New Moon and Sabbath and festivals and weekdays. Then the meditation of every heart and the offering of their voices shall ascend in favor before the Lord of all, and they shall be pleasing to God as in days of old, as is written, *May the words of my mouth and the meditation of my heart be acceptable to You, O Lord, my Rock and my Redeemer.*)

The noble story *The Parable and Its Lesson* is now complete.

NOTES

1   *Khmelnitski pogroms*   In 1648–49 the Cossack leader Bogdan Khmelnitski, as part of the uprising against the Polish Commonwealth, led a campaign of atrocities against Jews in the Ukraine. Jews were prime targets of Cossack fury because they were agents of the Polish aristocracy, who hired them to manage their estates. As many as tens of thousands of Jews were murdered and many communities were destroyed. The massacres were deeply rooted in the collective memory of Ashkenazic Jewry until the Holocaust overshadowed them. In Jewish annalistic literature Khmelnitski is often referred to as "Khmiel."

2   *through which his soul passes*   The idea that a name contains the essence of a person has its roots in Kabbalistic doctrine, as does the notion of *gilgul neshamot* (lit. the cycle of souls), in which the soul of a person cycles through a series of bodily incarnations over time.

6   *weekly Torah portion Mishpatim*   The weekly Torah portion comprising Exodus 21:1–24:18.

6   *portion of Ha'azinu*   The weekly Torah portion comprising Deuteronomy 32.

6   *the passage haniglot vehanistarot*   Lit. "*The revealed and the hidden. . . .*" These words occur in Deuteronomy 29:28. The authorized Hebrew (Masoretic) text of this verse contains eleven dots above these words and above the first letter of the word that follows. The origin and import of these dots is the subject of both scholarly speculation and midrashic interpretation. The JPS TANAKH renders the verse "Concealed acts concern the Lord our God; but with overt acts, it is for us and our children ever to apply all the provisions of this Teaching."

6   *the piyyut Unetanneh tokef*   A *piyyut* is a liturgical poem. The piyyut referred to here, *Unetanneh tokef* (Let Us Declare the Holiness of the Day), is recited during the Musaf service on Rosh Hashanah and Yom Kippur. Though its origins are earlier, the present text was written by the eleventh-century poet Kalonymus ben Meshullam Kalonymus of Mainz, Germany. Legend attributes it to one Amnon of Mainz, who is said to have composed it as he was being martyred by the local bishop for refusing to convert to Christianity. Three days after his death, so the story goes, he appeared to Kalonymus in a dream and taught him the poem.

7   *prayer recited upon*   Called in Hebrew *tefillat haderekh*, it is traditionally recited by travelers as they set out on a journey.

8   *seven nuptial benedictions*   Seven benedictions are chanted at the marriage ceremony and at the ensuing wedding feast. During the week following the

wedding, tradition mandates that a festive meal for the newlyweds be held each day. At the end of each meal, following the Grace, the seven benedictions are repeated. In order to ensure that the blessings remain fresh, it is customary to make sure there is present at each of the meals at least one "new face," i.e., someone who did not attend either the wedding ceremony or any of the previous meals. If there is not, the seven benedictions are not recited, except for the blessing over a cup of wine at the conclusion of the Grace after the meal.

8   *Kiddushin*   The talmudic tractate that treats the laws of betrothal.

8   *tractate Ḥagigah*   *Kaftor vaferaḥ* is a Hebrew treatise on rabbinic aggadah by Yaakov bar Yitzchak Luzzato, Safed, ca. 1527–1587. In the Lemberg, 1891 edition, the tale is found on p. 66a. The talmudic tractate Ḥagigah deals with the laws of the festival sacrifices.

8   *Aaron began to inquire*   It is unclear exactly what kind of inquiry Aaron is engaging in or who he is reading. Clearly it involves the philosophical speculation about first things and the problem of evil that was prevalent in the late seventeenth century.

9   *qelipot*   Lit. shells or husks. The reference is to the complex notion in Lurianic Kabbalah of "the breaking of the vessels." *Qelipot* signify the impurity and grossness that adhere to a person living in the unredeemed cosmos.

11   *Behukotai*   The Torah portion comprising Leviticus 26:3–27:34, generally read during May.

12   *melamed*   One who teaches Torah to children.

12   *banned by the community*   The reference is to *niddui*, a temporary ban (as opposed to excommunication) that could be imposed by the rabbinic authorities to ostracize and discipline a recalcitrant member of the community. The practice goes back to rabbinic times but with modifications was applied by later Jewish communities. It has currency today only in ultra-Orthodox communities.

13   *Fear no man*   Deuteronomy 1:17.

13   *Rabbenu Tam's tefillin*   Jewish law records a debate between Rashi (1040–1105) and his grandson, Rabbi Jacob Tam (usually referred to as Rabbenu Tam, ca. 1100–1171), over the order in which the parchments containing passages from the Torah are to be positioned inside the tefillin fitted on the head. Jews who are fastidious about the observance of this precept will don both Rashi and Rabbenu Tam tefillin on weekday mornings.

13   *Mountains of Darkness*   See Babylonian Talmud tractate Tamid 32b: "The

Tanna de-be Eliyahu taught: Gehinnom is above the firmament; some, however, say that is behind the Mountains of Darkness."

14 *Sabbath of Repentance* The Sabbath of Repentance (Hebrew, Shabbat *Shuvah*) is the Sabbath between Rosh Hashanah and Yom Kippur. Its name derives from the opening words of the prophetic reading that follows the Torah reading at the morning service: "*Shuvah yisra'el*" (Return, O Israel, to the LORD your God; Hosea 14:2.) It was customary on that Sabbath for the rabbi to present a major discourse or sermon on the theme of repentance to prepare the congregants for Yom Kippur.

15 *Israel in the desert* See Exodus 13:21ff., 40:34ff., Numbers 9:15–23.

16 *Shas* A Hebrew acronym for (1) *shomer sefarim*, which has the sense of book collector or bibliophile; and (2) "*shishah sedarim*" (six orders or parts), a Hebrew designation for the Mishnah, which contains six volumes. The term is used more broadly to denote the many tomes that contain the elaboration of the Mishnah in the sixty-three tractates of the Babylonian Talmud.

16 *Akdamut hymn* Composed by Meir ben Isaac Nehorai (eleventh century, northern France). The ninety-line *piyyut* is read by Ashkenazic Jews at the morning service on Shavuot just prior to the reading from the Torah.

17 *Gehinnom has seven names* Babylonian Talmud, tractate 'Eruvin 19a.

18 *twentieth of Sivan* The day on which the Jewish community of Nemirov was destroyed in the Cossack uprising of 1648. It came to be designated as a minor fast day to mark all the Khmelnitski massacres. In the Middle Ages Rabbi Jacob Tam designated the same date as a day of mourning for the Jews burned alive in the blood libel in Blois, France, in 1171.

18 *Strypa* A tributary of the Dniester river in Galicia, now western Ukraine, on which Buczacz is located.

18 *tashlikh ritual* The water used for making Passover matzah must be "water that has stood overnight," such that the dough will be sufficiently cool so as not to make it ferment quickly. The water must be drawn by a Jew from a river or well, placed in a clean vessel, and allowed to stand overnight or at least for twelve hours. *Tashlikh* (casting away) is the ritual performed on Rosh Hashanah afternoon or in the days following, in which one's sins are symbolically cast away into a naturally flowing body of water.

19 *My beloved knocks* Song of Songs 5:2.

19 *for Thou art with me* Psalm 23:4.

20 *from the hollow of the sling* The reference here is to the Babylonian Talmud,

tractate Shabbat 152b, where the two parts of a biblical verse (1 Samuel 25:29) are cited and interpreted: "R. Eliezer said, `The souls of the righteous are ensconced beneath the heavenly throne, as it is written, *May the soul of my lord be bound up in the bundle of life in the care of the Lord.* But the souls of the wicked are perpetually confined [to the hollow of a sling] and an angel stands at one end of the universe and another angel stands at the other end of the universe and they sling the souls [of the wicked back and forth] to one another, as it is written, *But He will fling the souls of your enemies as from the hollow of a sling'.*"

21   *Ari*   Acronymic name of Rabbi Isaac Luria (1534–1572), Jewish mystic and a major theorist of Kabbalah.

21   *raising up the souls*   The four letters of the Hebrew word *mishnah* can be transposed to the word *neshamah* (soul).

23   *the Kanah and the Peli'ah*   *Sefer ha-peli'ah* and *Sefer hakanah* are works of cosmogonic and theosophic speculation. Their authorship is uncertain, as are their date and country of origin. Some scholars place them in Spain of the late fourteenth century. Both works are marked by a strong antinomian strain.

23   *will find the door open to him*   Babylonian Talmud tractate Menaḥot 29b and in other places with variants.

23   *what will be in the end*   The allusion is to Mishnah Ḥagigah 2:1: "Whoever gives his mind to four things, it were better for him had he not come into this world: what is above, what is beneath, what was beforetime, and what will be in the hereafter."

24   *the superhuman sons of God*   See Genesis 6:1–4.

24   *over the surface of the deep*   Genesis 1:2.

24   *the domain of the qelipot*   Elhanan Shilo, in a private correspondence, notes that Agnon's language here is citing Naftali Bacharach in his book expositing Lurianic Kabbakah, *Emek hamelekh*, 16:11.

24   *induced its curse within him*   See Numbers 5:11–31, where the procedure prescribed for a woman suspected of adultery is detailed.

24   *and an inner one*   Otzar hamidrashim, 'olam katan, no. 4.

25   *to sleep in one's house all alone*   Babylonian Talmud tractate Shabbat 151b.

26   *from transgression, says the Lord*   Isaiah 59:20.

27   *his share in the world to come*   Babylonian Talmud tractates Bava Metziah 59a and Sanhedrin 107a.

28   *than the flights of desire*   Ecclesiastes 6:9.

28   *a compartment they call Tsalmavet*   The idea that Gehinnom is composed

of different compartments is found in the Babylonian Talmud tractates Sotah 10b and 'Eruvin 19a.

28   *larger than Earth*   Job 11:9.

29   *wrapped in silver-crowned talitot*   Exodus 12:37 and Numbers 11:21 report that 600,000 adult males went forth from Egypt. This number is made more precise in the censuses noted in Exodus 38:26 and Numbers 1:46, where the figure given is 603,550 adult males. Accordingly, when women and children are added, the total of those who left Egypt would be over two million. Thus the number of people implied here is astronomical.

29   *chief rabbis and heads of yeshivot*   Chief rabbis or *Landesrabbiner* were regional head rabbis of districts and provinces in the countries of Central Europe. A Rosh Yeshivah is the head rabbi of a talmudical academy (Yeshivah).

29   *Sabbath boundary*   The Sabbath boundary (*teḥum shabbat*) is the distance beyond the defined city limits that one is permitted to walk on the Sabbath, stipulated in rabbinic sources as two thousand cubits or about three-quarters of a mile.

31   *has given to mankind*   Psalm 115:16.

31   *Otem*   This name comes from the Hebrew root *'atom*, to stop up, as in Proverbs 21:13 *Who stops his ears at the cry of the wretched.*

31   *what the living say*   Based on Babylonian Talmud tractate Berakhot 27b.

33   *their own compartment of Gehinnom*   See Midrash Ecclesiastes Rabbah 3:9 for the idea that individuals of like profession or vocation are assigned to their own particular compartment of Gehinnom.

33   *a candle of the Lord*   Proverbs 20:27.

34   *whose transgression is forgiven*   Psalm 32:2.

34   *forgives iniquity*   Exodus 34:6–7.

35   *cross through your land*   Leviticus 26:6.

35   *in accordance with Your word*   Psalm 119:28.

35   *in rumbling hordes*   After the Khmelnitski massacres of 1648, there were serious invasions of Galicia by Tatars and Turks in the 1670s.

36   *to get the atonement chickens*   The reference is to the *kaparot* (lit. expiations) ceremony performed by observant Jews on the morning of the day before Yom Kippur, in which the sins of an individual are symbolically transferred to a live fowl. The fowl—a rooster for a man, a hen for a woman—is swung around the head three times as biblical verses and a formula of vicarious atonement is recited. Money in the amount of the fowl's value is often substituted for the fowl.

36   *Book of the Angel Razi'el   Sefer Razi'el hamalakh*, an early medieval book of instruction in magical lore and practices written in Hebrew and derived from the Jewish mystical tradition (Kabbalah). Its precise date and authorship are uncertain.

36   *never asked anyone to get his staff for him*   Babylonian Talmud tractate Sotah 10a. The implication is that Samson not only did not take bribes *which blind the eyes of the wise* (Deuteronomy 16:19) but sought no favors of any kind from anyone.

36   *recited the Torah blessings*   In the morning regimen, after the hands are washed and before the service proper, three short blessings concerning the giving and the study of Torah are recited, followed by readings from the Written Law (the Priestly blessing, Numbers 6:24–26) and the Oral Law (Mishnah Pe'ah 1:1) and the preliminary morning blessings.

37   *who crowns Israel in glory*   One of the blessings preliminary to the morning service. The letters on the parchments inside the tefillin are, like those on the Torah scroll, typically embellished by the scribe with tiny filigreed crowns over them.

37   *talmudic tractate Yevamot*   A key source for many of the laws pertaining to an agunah.

37   *lasts for twelve months*   As stated by Rabbi Akiva in Mishnah 'Eduyot 2:10.

37   *worse than the heat of the sun*   These details of Gehinnom are drawn from various midrashic sources.

39   *young men and women*   Psalm 148:12.

40   *area forbidden to kohanim*   A *kohen* is required by Jewish law to remain in a state of ritual purity. Physical presence near a corpse or in a cemetery defiles him.

40   *implored the Lord*   Exodus 32:11. On public fast days at the afternoon service, the prescribed reading from the Torah is Exodus 32:11–14 and 34:1–10. The *haftarah* (reading from the prophetic books of the Bible) is Isaiah 55:6–56:8.

40   *to those already gathered*   Isaiah 56:8.

41   *resembled a silver goblet*   Agnon is drawing here on the kabbalistic notion that the whiteness or the darkness of one's hair reflects the nature and quality of the inner self. See Elhanan Shilo, *Hakabbalah biyetsirat Shai 'Agnon* [The Kabbalah in the Works of S. Y. Agnon] Ramat Gan: Bar Ilan University Press, 2011, Hebrew), p. 223ff.

42   *there had been much persecution*   See above, note to page 16. Popular legend has it that Meir ben Isaac miraculously saved the Jewish community of Worms, and the *Akdamut* piyyut commemorates the event.

43   *Tosafot note in tractate Gittin*   The talmudic tractate Gittin treats of the

laws of divorce. Zevaḥim treats of the animal sacrifices offered in the Temple. The Rashi comment is found at Zevaḥim 45b. The Tosafot note is at Gittin 54b.

44   *of My servant Moses*   Malachi 3:22.

44   *in the Book of the Angel Razi'el   Sefer Razi'el hamalakh* (Warsaw, n.d.), p. 22. Cited in Shilo, *Hakabbalah biyetsirat Shai 'Agnon*, p. 321 note 107.

44   *sacrifical offering in the Temple*   The *Tamid* offering, described in Numbers 28:1–8.

45   *pray the whole day long*   Babylonian Talmud tractate Berakhot 21a.

46   *standing here with me*   Deuteronomy 5:28.

46   *shall a case be established*   Deuteronomy 19:15.

46   *punishment for our transgressions*   The reference is to Isaiah 40:2.

48   *midrash on Songs of Songs*   Midrash Rabbah on Song of Songs 1:8. Some versions have a different numbering.

48   *Midrash Tanhuma*   A collection of rabbinic midrash in several versions, dating uncertain.

49   *It is prayer*   Babylonian Talmud tractate Ta'anit 2a. The biblical verses respectively are from Exodus 23:25 and Deuteronomy 11:13. The reference to Maimonides is a verbatim citation from his *Mishneh Torah*, the Laws of Prayer, 1.1.

49   *mandated by the Torah itself*   Naḥmanides (R. Moses ben Naḥman, Ramban, 1194–1270) was a major Bible commentator and halakhist. Maimonides' *Book of the Commandments* (*Sefer hamizvot*) is a detailed catalogue of the 248 positive and 365 negative commandments on which Naḥmanides wrote critical glosses, this being among the most famous.

49   *from the right earlock of the great teacher*   In Lurianic Kabbalah, the earlocks are metaphysical signifiers, the right one associated with the holy and the mystical, the left one with the mundane and the philosophical. Thus is Naḥmanides, a kabbalist, privileged over Maimonides. See Shiloh, *Hakabbalah biyetsirat Shai 'Agnon*, pp. 226–228.

50   *Gates of Light   Sha'arei 'orah*, a kabbalistic treatise by Joseph ben Abraham Gikatilla (1248–ca. 1305), Fifth Gate, Sixth Sphere.

50   *Midrash ha-ne'elam*   The Esoteric Midrash—a kabbalistic text inserted into the main text of the Zohar.

50   *Pirke de Rabbi Eliezer*   A late rabbinic midrash on Genesis, Exodus, and other parts of the Bible. It is ascribed to R. Eliezer ben Hyrcanus (late first, early second century) but is dated to the seventh or eighth century. The reference here is to the explication of Genesis 32:27ff. in chapter 37.

50   *his fragrance rubbed off on my hand*   Talmudic tractate Zevaḥim 96b. The folk saying conveys the idea that one acquires luster through association with an eminent person.

51   *knows its own bitterness*   Proverbs 14:10.

51   *the reward of humility is grace*   An adaptation of Proverbs 22:4.

51   *to the children of Israel*   Leviticus 23:44.

52   *and your father's house*   Psalm 45:11.

52   *never laid eyes on*   Despite the centrality of Torah study, full sets of the Babylonian Talmud were not then necessarily widely available because of the cost. It is, therefore, not unimaginable for someone not to have seen ʿEruvin, which is not among the more commonly learned talmudic tractates. The tractate deals with the laws of *ʿeruv*, the halakhic extension of private property into the public domain so as to permit one to carry objects within it on the Sabbath, which would otherwise be forbidden.

52   *could view the minor tractates*   Tractates of rabbinic teachings on subjects not treated in the Mishnah. They are usually included at the back of some volumes in printed editions of the Babylonian Talmud.

52   *weekly Torah portion was Yitro*   Exodus 18–20. The Decalogue is at 20:1–14.

52   *the Ten Commandments in Deuteronomy*   Deuteronomy 5:6–18, the second iteration of the Decalogue in the Pentateuch.

53   *with their children forever*   Deuteronomy 5:26.

54   *how feeble our strength*   Jeremiah 51:30.

54   *study its ways and learn*   Proverbs 30:25 and 6:6.

54   *who dwell in your House*   Psalm 84:2–5.

54   *will die with my nest*   Job 29:18.

54   *all the days of my life*   Psalm 23:6.

54   *would only cite Rabbi Ibn Ezra*   Rabbi Abraham Ibn Ezra (1089–1164), Spanish grammarian and Bible commentator.

54   *the Radak*   Rabbi David Kimḥi (1160–1235), Provençal grammarian and Bible commentator.

55   *who have been banished*   Psalm 113:3 and 2 Samuel 14:14.

55   *passing shadow*   Psalm 144:4.

56   *and trample My courts*   Isaiah 1:12.

56   *who call upon him in truth*   Psalm 145:18.

57   *blame will not be lacking*   An adaptation of Proverbs 10:19 *Where there is much talk, there is no lack of transgression.*

57   *afflicted, downtrodden, and hurting*   Talmudic tractate Yevamot 47a.

57   *will put an end to words*   Job 18:1.

57   *full-day fast of silence*   The practice of a "fast of speech," *Ta'anit dibbur*, arose only in early modern times as a penance and as a means to achieve greater spiritual elevation. It is not ordained biblically or rabbinically. The time for which it was undertaken varied, and during it the practitioner either kept silent or spoke only about Torah matters.

58   *between His shoulders*   Deuteronomy 33:12.

58   *Benjamin is a ravenous wolf*   Genesis 49:27.

58–59   *sit alone and keep silent*   Lamentations 3:28.

60   *to make up the loss*   Moses Isserles (Rama), citing 'Or Zaru'a in *Shulḥan Arukh*, *'Or hahayyim* 135:2.

60   *moment of truth*   After 2 Chronicles 32:1.

60   *charges with folly*   Job 4:18.

61   *utters in Perek Shira*   *Perek Shira* (Passages of Praise) is a poemlike collection of biblical and talmudic verses of praise to God placed in the figurative mouths of the heavenly bodies; the elements of the natural world; the various members of the vegetable, animal, bird, and insect kingdoms; and, as indicated here, Gehinnom. The text appears in authoritative editions of the prayerbook but is not part of the liturgy. Author and date are unknown, but the work may go back to talmudic times.

61   *from one end of the world to the other*   *Otzar hamidrashim, Gan 'Eden/Gehinnom* no. 32.

61   *rest on that day*   *Otzar hamidrashim, 'Aseret hadibrot* no. 10.

61   *judged for twelve months*   Mishnah 'Eduyot 2.10.

61   *does not descend again*   Babylonian Talmud tractate Shabbat 153a.

61   *fiery glow of Gehinnom*   Talmudic tractate Ḥagigah 27a.

62   *ascribe truth to Jacob*   Micah 7:20.

63   *from the commandment to study Torah*   Agnon cites this teaching in his *Sefer sippur vesofer* (p. 105, 108 in new ed.), citing Nathan ben Isaac Jacob Bonn's *Shikḥehat leket* (Amsterdam, 1700), who attributes it to the *Sodei razaya* of Eliezer of Worms (ca. 1176–1238, author of the Rokeah).

64   *blessings on behalf of each individual*   At the conclusion of each section of the Torah reading (aliyah), the gabbai recites a blessing on behalf of the person called to the Torah for that section, as well as for his wife, family, and any other individuals he chooses to name. The blessing includes the sum of money the person stipulates

to the gabbai as his pledge to the synagogue for the honor of having been called to the Torah reading.

65   *gematria calculation*   Gematria involves adding up the numerical value of each letter of the Hebrew alphabet (alef = 1, bet = 2, etc.). Eighteen is the numerical value of the two letters in the word *ḥai*, the Hebrew word for life; twenty-six is the numerical value of the four letters of the Tetragrammaton.

65   *beats her laundry to get the water out*   The term is probably related to *pralnia*, the Polish word for laundry.

65   *as I have told elsewhere*   See *'Ir umelo'ah*, pp. 1ff. and 15.

65   *Rabbi Meshullam ben Kalonymus*   Rabbi Gershom (ca. 960–1028) and Rabbi Shimon (ca. 925–1010) were important rabbinical authorities in Mainz, a major Jewish community in the medieval Rhineland (Ashkenaz). Rabbi Meshullam ben Kalonymus (Italy, mid-tenth century) was a Talmudist and liturgical poet who corresponded with Gershom and Shimon on halakhic and scientific matters.

66   *our God stands firm forever*   Isaiah 40:8.

66   *gives tongue to knowledge*   Proverbs 16:21.

66   *to the local maskilim*   The *maskilim* (lit. enlightened ones, sing. *maskil*) referred to here are the literati in the Jewish community of that time who had some notion of secular ideas and books beyond classical Jewish sources. They antedate and anticipate their namesakes of the eighteenth and nineteenth centuries, who formally espoused the values of the Enlightenment (*Haskalah* in Hebrew). See above, note to page 8 (*Aron began . . .*).

66   *and knowing Me*   Jeremiah 9:23.

66   *who seeks after God*   Psalms 14:2 and 53:3.

68   *my Rock and my Redeemer*   Psalm 19:15.

ESSAY ON *THE PARABLE AND ITS LESSON* [*HAMASHAL VEHANIMSHAL*]

ALAN MINTZ

THE WORK OF MEMORY

Within the panoply of modern Jewish writing, Shmuel Yosef Agnon remains today an exceptional presence. At the center of the grand narrative of Jewish literature in our age is the movement outward from the world of the fathers. Whether the goal is full participation in American culture or the building of a new Jewish society in Palestine, the movement outward presupposes a break with the metaphysics of traditional Jewish belief and practice. That break can be figured as a clear-eyed ideological rejection or as a vertiginous loss of moorings, or as a sloughing off of a used-up identity. Whatever the case, the claims of Jewish law and the textual and theological world on which it is founded are stilled and suspended. The possibility of return continues to exist, and from time to time there appears a Rosenzweig who, out of the depths of acculturation, discovers the mystique of a Judaism he never knew. In relation to all these varied trajectories, Agnon's exceptionality becomes clearer. Born into the world of tradition, Agnon found a way to participate in high European modernism without abandoning the rich textual world of Jewish faith. He even used this traditional world as a vehicle for realizing the ends of modernism at the same time as he used modernism as an instrument for illuminating fissures within the classical edifice of

Judaism. Agnon thus performed the paradox of being a "revolutionary traditionalist," in the formulation of Gershon Shaked.[1] Comprehending this singular accomplishment has become one of the great challenges of modern Jewish literary studies.

During the last fifteen years of his life (he died in 1970), Agnon became increasingly preoccupied with writing an epic cycle of stories about Buczacz, the town in Galicia in which he was raised and that he left at the age of nineteen to settle in Palestine. The stories were gathered and edited by his daughter Emunah Yaron, according to her father's guidelines, in 1973 in a volume called *'Ir umelo'ah, A City in Its Fullness.*[2] It is from this story cycle that *The Parable and Its Lesson* is drawn. The stories of *'Ir umelo'ah* give strong evidence for the existence of a late style in Agnon. I am using late style (*spätstil*) in the sense in which Theodor Adorno used the term to describe the late sonatas of Beethoven as works that constitute a "moment when the artist who is fully in command of his medium nevertheless abandons communication with the established social order of which he is part and achieves a contradictory, alienated relationship with it."[3] Edward Said adopts Adorno's notion and uses it less as a precise term than as an evocative concept for illuminating the regressive freedom from constraints that writers and composers might allow themselves in the last stages of their careers. In a similarly evocative and nontechnical sense, the idea of late style helps us attend to the departures enacted in Agnon's cycle of Buczacz stories. In Agnon's case, the late breakthrough manifests itself as an act of renunciation. One of Agnon's greatest achievements in the major phase of his career was an ironic self-dramatizing mode of narration that Arnold Band called the "dramatized ego."[4] The narrator of these important stories—as well as of the novel *Oreaḥ natah lalun* [A Guest for the Night]—is a figure very much like Agnon himself: a grandiose but weak-willed middle-aged writer with worldly interests as well as a loyalty to religious observance and Jewish learning, a kind of Jewish version of the *homme moyen sensuel.* Agnon used this persona to great advantage; but when it came to chronicling the long history of Buczacz he needed a narrative stance that, at least on the face of things, was objective, reliable and impersonal. And so he undertook the construction of the narrator of *'Ir umelo'ah*, who is a fascinating and formidable and new figure, but one whose creation meant putting away and giving up the authorial strategies relied on for so long.

Now, one might have expected a thunderous reception for a major book published three years after the death of a major author, especially if the author was the only Hebrew writer to have been awarded the Nobel Prize for Literature, as Agnon was in 1966, together with Nelly Sachs. Yet the response in Israel's vibrant literary community was decidedly scant and muted; the book was hardly noticed, and those who wrote about it tended to be older critics who were already possessed of a long-term devotion to Agnon's work. There are several factors that might account for this surprising failure to connect to an audience. To begin with, the stories in *'Ir umelo'ah*, all of which have to do with the lives of Galician Jews in the pre-modern period, describe a world that must have seemed remote, antiquated and irrelevant in the decades of intense state building after the War of Independence. Within the Zionist consensus about the untenable nature of Jewish life in exile, there had always been room for literary depictions that exposed the inner moral taint and political vulnerability of diaspora life. Even though the Buczacz stories convey no small measure of those failings, they nevertheless present a picture of a vital semi-autonomous and centuries-old religious communal culture; and this image could not have comported well with the attitudes and judgments of David Ben-Gurion's statism and the society it shaped. During these years Ben-Gurion was busy building a state, while Agnon was building a city.

A second factor was the implied judgment that within Agnon's overall artistic career *'Ir umelo'ah* represented a regression. Agnon had acceded to the status of a great European modernist with the publication of the parabolic stories of *Sefer hama'ayinasim* [Book of Deeds] and *Temol shilshom* [Only Yesterday, 1945], a novel of the Second Aliyah with its brilliantly surreal passages written in the voice of a supposedly mad dog named Balak. For readers who esteemed Agnon for these achievements, the Buczacz stories seemed a throwback to a more naïve and less accomplished artist who had become sentimental in old age and renounced the ironic lens through which his best work was filtered. The decline and decimation of Buczacz had already been critically analyzed in the great pre-war novel *Oreaḥ natah lalun* [A Guest for the Night, 1939], and now, after the Holocaust completed the work of destruction, it was felt that Agnon was producing something very different: a *yizker bukh*, a memorial volume suffused with nostalgia and mourning for a lost world. Finally, the unique qualities of *'Ir umelo'ah* were obscured within the plethora of titles published within the years following the author's death.[5] This posthumous Agnon corpus, whose volumes in their original editions are distinguished by their black dust jackets and white bindings, amounts to fourteen titles, some of which appeared in close succession. Among the lot are thematic anthologies of classical sources, collections of correspondence and gatherings of public statements and occasional speeches, as well as fiction.[6] The most sensational of these publications was the appearance in 1971 of the novel *Shira*, a tale of marital infidelity set among German émigré scholars in Jerusalem of the 1930s. Chapters of the novel published in 1948 had whetted the appetite of an eager readership, but out of a scruple of discretion, Agnon had made provision for the appearance of the whole novel only after his death, and the estimation of the stir it would cause was not off the mark.[7] When *'Ir umelo'ah* appeared two years later, fragmentary epic of a vanished world that it is, there was little critical oxygen remaining.

'Ir umelo'ah, I would argue, is one of the most extraordinary responses to the murder of European Jewry in modern Jewish writing, yet the very connection of the work to the Holocaust is fraught and not entirely self-evident. On the one hand, the book as a whole is dedicated—on a separate page following the title page—to a city that flourished from the time of its founding "until the arrival of the vile, defiled and depraved enemy, and the madmen who abetted them, and brought about utter annihilation." On the other hand, neither the Nazi liquidations nor even the rehearsal for them in World War One is represented in the stories, which do not reach beyond the nineteenth century. So despite the fact the sto-

ries are occasionally punctuated with invective against the Nazis and their role in bringing about the end of Jewish Buczacz, anything related to that destruction is kept from the representational field of the work. The potential for confusion created by this paradox can be illustrated, with the reader's indulgence, by a personal testimony. Many years ago, when I was planning the research that led to my *Ḥurban: Responses to Catastrophe in Hebrew Literature*, I was examining Israeli literature for reactions to the Holocaust. Of course, I looked first to Agnon as the preeminent Hebrew writer who, unlike many of his Israeli counterparts, did not turn away from the diaspora and its religious culture. Yet, apart from several unconnected stories, I saw little at the time that would dissuade me from the conclusion that the literary world of the master was fixed in its characteristic modalities in the decades before the Holocaust and that a substantial reorientation toward the catastrophe could not be expected. It is clear to me now that I was wrong. What blinded me was a narrow conception of what it means to respond to catastrophe. To qualify as such, I mistakenly believed that a work of literature must represent the horrors of destruction, as well as depicting modes of survival and reconstruction. Because Agnon had not engaged the horrors, his work could not be thought of in any substantial sense as being part of Holocaust literature.

Reading *'Ir umelo'ah* has taught me three things. First, contending with the burden of the Holocaust was exactly what Agnon was doing in the postwar decades. The crucial story "Hasiman" [The Sign], which Emunah Yaron placed at the conclusion of *'Ir umelo'ah*, is actually a consecration story that introduces the project as a whole.[8] The story describes the holiday of Shavuot in the Jerusalem suburb of Talpiyot in 1943, when the narrator, a stand-in for the author, is informed about the murder of the Jews of Buczacz. Late that night in the synagogue, the narrator undergoes a mystical experience in which the great medieval poet Solomon Ibn Gabirol appears to him and composes a sacred poem to perpetuate the memory of the Jews of Buczacz. The implication is that the narrator, who is deeply connected to the tradition of liturgical poetry, will now take this burden on himself and continue the task of memorialization is his own, storytelling mode. The epic cycle of Buczacz stories that took shape in these years is a direct result of that self-imposed imperative.

Second, Agnon makes a principled choice not to traffic in atrocity and instead devote his resources to reimagining the spiritual life of Galician Jewry in its fullest vigor. In a profound sense, those spiritual achievements were decimated long before the Nazis arrived on the scene; the twin forces of secularization and the terrors of World War One and the Russian Civil War saw to that. The Holocaust was the satanic coup de grace that provided a tragic point of retrospection for taking stock of Buczacz and all it represented in the centuries of its greatness when, as the narrator so often observes in *'Ir umelo'ah*, "Buczacz was Buczacz." This reimagining is aware of itself as a literary endeavor, an artifice that knows it cannot bring back the dead or replace them. At the same time, it makes the claim that it is within the capabilities of the literary imagination to create a simulacrum of the fullness of that lost world, and that this act of creation/re-creation, both in its process and its product, is the true response we must make to catastrophe.

Finally, Agnon's practice in *'Ir umelo'ah* has within it the power to require us to rethink our most basic notions about Holocaust literature. It has been axiomatic for many that the chief vocation of Holocaust literature is to represent the unspeakable ordeals that were visited upon the murdered victims, the survivors and their children. Without necessarily negating this mode of representation, Agnon declines to pursue it in favor of the imaginative reconstruction of an earlier lost spiritual and cultural plenitude. His motives, I would argue, derive from a deep intuition into the demands Jewish tradition makes on the modern imagination. In addition to giving voice to grief in the form of lamentation, the classical tradition stressed over time the recouping of the relationship between God and Israel and the restoration and repurification of the image of the destroyed community.[9] In a modern era, this restorative impulse works through the literary imagination and takes the form of storytelling. Agnon retells the story of Buczacz as an imperfect but holy community, a *qehilah qedoshah*. His approach underscores the significance of cultural frameworks in determining responses to the Holocaust.[10] Putting complex matters simply, we may say that an exclusive focus on extermination, atrocity and the death-in-life of survivors presents the Holocaust as the final vitiation of Enlightenment European culture. Focusing instead on the substance of the religious-cultural civilization of the past, even if the integrity of that civilization was severely compromised by the time of its destruction, presents the Holocaust as a rupture within the internal relations of the Jewish people and its history.

But does not such an imaginative program of restitution inevitably lead to an idealization of the lost object? And does the idealization of the past serve or traduce creative survival in the future? A famous example of this kind of response is Nathan Nata Hanover's *Yeven metsulah* [Abyss of Despair], a chronicle of the sufferings of Polish Jewry during the Khmelnitski massacres of 1648–49.[11] After a martyrologically tinged account of the horrific ordeals suffered by the Jewish communities of Galicia and the Ukraine, Hanover concludes his work with a eulogy that mourns the greatness that was once Polish Jewry; the slaughtered communities are collectively recalled as systematically embodying the cardinal virtues of Torah, *avodah* and *ma'asim tovim*. Agnon is especially aware of Hanover's chronicle because the consequences of the Khmelnitski massacres play so important a role in the history of Buczacz. Yet when it comes to mounting his own project of remembrance, the option of composing an idyll is one Agnon conspicuously declines. Although idealization is not absent from *'Ir umelo'ah*, it is reconfigured to serve a different purpose. Memorialization, for Agnon, is a set of critical choices and discriminations. In *'Ir umelo'ah*, it is synagogue worship and Torah study that become the signs under which Agnon will set about reimagining the history of Buczacz. It is important to keep in mind that this was only one among a number of schemata Agnon could have chosen. The past could have been recouped around Jewish-gentile relations, or the economic fortunes of the various handicrafts and trades that flourished in the town, or relations between the poor and prosperous. It may seem natural that Agnon would have chosen worship and study, but it remains a choice.

'Ir umelo'ah begins with a description of the town's study houses and synagogues, their appurtenances and sacred objects and then proceeds to a consideration of the key personalities who held the offices of ḥazzan (cantor), shamash (sexton, beadle), and gabbai (treasurer); accounts of the great rabbis who held sway in Buczacz, as well as tales of anonymous piety, occupy the core of the book. Yet this plan is only a scaffolding; it represents the idealizing framework within which Agnon chooses to perform the memory of Buczacz and present his town in the largest possible way as inscribed within the world of Torah. Woven in and out of this scaffolding, however, are innumerable accounts of professional and scholarly jealousy, internecine commercial rivalries, unchecked acts of cruelty and expropriation by the wealthy, unrewarded acts of righteousness by the poor and lowly, apostasy, criminality, suicide and many other unsavory behaviors.

As conjured up by Agnon in *'Ir umelo'ah*, the vanished world of Buczacz can best be understood under the rubric of a norm and deviations from it. Agnon sets the value signature of the work, chooses the periods in the life of Buczacz in which Torah and worship are paramount, fashions a plan for the organization of the stories that foregrounds these institutions and their practitioners and uses the commentary of the volume's ever-present narrator to articulate and reinforce this moral framework. Yet at the same time, the norm is continually flouted by power, envy and the general intractability of the human heart. *'Ir umelo'ah* is a world in which there is a single moral and spiritual norm alongside an abundance of variegated deviations from that norm. It will not come as a surprise that the deviations more often beguile the reader's attention than does the norm, and the modal tension between the two accounts for the fascination exerted by the book and for the tensile forces that hold it together.

Holding together a work made up of more than 140 independent narrative units is not a small challenge. Of the several strategies Agnon uses in his efforts to create coherence in *'Ir umelo'ah*, the most important is the fashioning of a narrator whose voice is present in almost all the stories. Surely this narrator is one of Agnon's greatest and most distinctive creations, and its arrival on the scene so late in the master's career has much to tell us about the aesthetic impasses he faced and the solutions he was experimenting with in the years after the war. The narrator of *'Ir umelo'ah* is part chronicler and part impresario. As chronicler, he presents himself as an assiduous student of the history of Buczacz and the arcana of its centuries of spiritual life. He takes advantage of every chance to establish the reliability of his accounts of events in terms of both the accuracy of his information and the objectivity with which it is presented. But make no mistake: although he takes pains to get his facts correct and puncture fanciful myths and legends, this chronicler is not a historian. He is a believing Jew who, though fully aware of the modern world, remains rooted in the circle of traditional piety. He views his function as a belated extension of the *pinqas*, the register kept by Jewish communities in Europe in which significant events were recorded.[12] At the conclusion of *Hamashal vehanimshal* [*The Parable and Its Lesson*], the story to be discussed below, the rationale for telling the lengthy tale is based on the fact that the *pinqas* of Buczacz was destroyed in the war along with the town's Jews. The extraordinary incidents related in the story were recorded there around the year 1700 in the beautiful hand of the town's scribe and in the formal eloquence of learned, biblical Hebrew.

It is now left to the belated narrator to reconstruct and retell the story as best he can and according to his own lights. He is not a communal scribe, but he does follow after the scribe, in his footsteps, as it were, in discharging the same function but using a different set of instruments. In his role as chronicler, most importantly, the narrator takes the prerogative to speak as an *I* that is simultaneously a *We*. He is himself first and foremost a man of Buczacz, flesh of the flesh of the town, although he has no historical embodiment that would locate him in actual events. He is at once absorbed into the collective conscience of the town *and* busily conducting the performance of memory under his own baton, a baton singularly inscribed with the proprietary pronoun *I*, if not with a proper name. It goes without saying, however, that by choosing to write about Buczacz in its "classic" era Agnon renounced his right to evoke personal childhood memories, as he did in such wonderful stories as "Hamitpaḥat" [The Kerchief], and, as pointed out above, to assimilate the figure of the narrator to his own autobiographical persona as he had done in *Oreaḥ natah lalun* [A Guest for the Night].

The narrator is also an impresario of memory who hosts or stages the voices of others, even while he remains on stage. In *Hamashal vehanimshal*, for example, most of the story is given over to the tale told by the old shamash. It is the narrator who sets up the frame story and describes the provocation that sets the story about the tour of Hell in motion, and it is he who returns toward the end to convey its effects on the community. But the greater duration of the story is given over to the shamash's own account of these extraordinary happenings. This hand-off, however, is not accomplished with complete serenity. Even though the crusty and acerbic attitudes of the old man set his voice apart as uniquely his, the narrator periodically expresses anxiety lest the two voices, his and the shamash's, be confused. Throughout *'Ir umelo'ah* the narrator is busy and in control and highly self-aware of the decisions he is making to follow up one story line over another and whether to allow himself a particular digression—which he usually does—or hew to a linear presentation of plot. The presence of the narrator is felt as constantly exerting an executive agency.

The narrator's most conspicuous endowment is his omniscience. The narrator speaks from the present. It is, after all, the unspeakable news of the Holocaust that moves him to undertake telling the story of Buczacz. At the same time, however, the periods of the town's history he has chosen to chronicle are not those about which he can have personal or eyewitness knowledge. *'Ir umelo'ah* focuses on a two-hundred-year span from the middle of the seventeenth century to the middle of the nineteenth. Even by using oral traditions and written records, no one could reasonably aspire to the omniscience the narrator claims for himself. This is exactly the nonrealistic, even magical, premise that Agnon lays down for the fundamental device that organizes his project. The narrator is

a construct that is defined as a sapient, nonpersonal entity that has attained an exhaustive grasp of the history of Buczacz. His conscience is
the repository of the *pinqasim* of the town for scores of generations. A
man of faith loyal to the core norms of study and worship, he has no
interest in history per se, that is, history in the modern, critical sense of
the term.

But he is passionately concerned about accuracy, and most of the
asides and introductions and commentaries in which we hear his voice
are preoccupied with asserting the reliability of his reporting and the
authority of his knowledge. This is no pallid conception of reliability.
The narrator knows what two characters said to each other, in their
exact words, in a private conversation in the late seventeenth century;
he knows what is in the heart of a merchant about to approach a Polish lord with a daring commercial proposition; he knows the text of the
offer of rabbinic appointment that failed to lure a luminary to Buczacz;
and he knows not only the desires of a poor yeshiva student but also the
thoughts of the great fish he is transporting to a demanding gourmand.
When he is not sure of a detail—say, whether it was eight coins or ten
that were paid for a wagon ride 250 years ago—he readily admits his
uncertainty and thereby implies that his authority on all matters not so
stipulated is utterly trustworthy.

Take this example from the beginning of *Hamashal vehanimshal*:

> There was in our beit midrash an old shamash named Reb Yeruham
> ben Tanhum. Some insist that his name was Reb Tanhum ben Yeruham
> and that it was in the Great Synagogue was where he served. Then there
> are those who claim that this name belongs not to the shamash but to
> the man who got involved with the him. I, who know only the names
> of those who served as shamash in the ten generations before I left my
> hometown, cannot make this determination. I can only tell the story.

Rather than being a genuine confession of limitation, the fuzziness about
the exact name and the exact place serves as a gesture of humility whose
purpose is to make the opposite point. Despite the fact that the strange

adventure that is about to be described in great detail took place well beyond ten generations ago, these few facts at the beginning of the story are the *only* ones to which any doubt attaches. And the very fact that these details are wrangled over with other, unnamed minds works only to strengthen the status of the events described in the story as indisputably part of the collective historical record.

Agnon is playing here at something very deep yet elusive. There is of course no rational world in which a narrator can possess such infinite knowledge. Yet as readers we are prepared to recognize omniscience as a legitimate convention when it comes to modern fiction. Not only do we not question Flaubert's right to represent Emma Bovary's innermost thoughts but we applaud his comprehensive penetration into her mind. And although Flaubert—a favorite of Agnon's—would claim his revelations of Emma's inner life to be true, he would also acknowledge them, proudly, as fiction. This is not the case with Agnon in *'Ir umelo'ah*. The texts of this collection are presented as stories, as *sipurim*, narratives that occupy a middle ground between chronicle and fiction; *sipur* is a supremely serviceable term for Agnon because it as much at home in the world of Hasidic piety as it is in the world of Kleist and Kafka. Yet his was not the short story perfected and aestheticized by Chekhov, Maupassant and Joyce but rather the kind of tale told by a storyteller in a world before the institutionalization of literature. In the case of *'Ir umelo'ah* the storyteller is not a primitive spinner of legends or folktales but a sophisticated and opinionated narrator-chronicler who curates and recirculates accounts of the key moments in the town's history and vouches for their accuracy. The pseudo-traditionalism of this form provided Agnon with a creative, flexible instrument. Although the narrator's values are aligned with the pious norms at the core of the stories, his responsibilities as a chronicler entail his reliable reporting of the full range of human behavior; and thus a gap is opened up that is at turns playful, ironic and subversive. In subtle and surreptitious ways, Agnon could appropriate the authenticity and authority of the traditional tale without renouncing the toolkit of modernism. Agnon thus wants—and gets—to have his literary cake and eat it too. He wants the freedom to imagine conversations, inner thoughts and the intimate particulars of behavior; and at the same time he denies that his stories are made up or lack the status of responsible accounts of historical occurrences. Agnon appropriates for himself a conception of storytelling that avoids the necessity of facing this either-or.

The path that Agnon fashioned in *'Ir umelo'ah* was a watershed in the master's relationship to the world he left behind as a youth. Setting aside for the moment the corpus of short stories, we note that Agnon wrote three novels between the world wars in which he attempted fictional reckonings with the exilic past. *Hakhnasat kalah* [The Bridal Canopy, 1931] is set in Galicia in the years before the Napoleonic wars and follows the wanderings of a holy fool who travels from town to town to raise money for his daughter's dowry. Although told by a pious narrator, the novel is rife with parody and social critique, and its plot is driven by conventions of the melodramatic novel; the hero's wanderings are used as an armature for an agglomeration of tales told at every station of his quest. *Sipur pashut* [A Simple Story, 1936], which takes place in Buczacz itself at the turn of the twentieth century, appropriates the conventions of the bourgeois family saga in the manner of Mann's *Buddenbrooks*, in telling the story of a young man in conflict between romantic love and the mercantile ethos of his family. In this recension of Buczacz, religion has been reduced to cultural patterning in the background, and the town is presented as a site of incipient class conflict. The narrator of *Oreaḥ natah lalun* [A Guest for the Night, 1939] bears a close resemblance to Agnon himself; he is a Jew from Palestine who has returned for a yearlong visit to Shibush (Buczacz), the town of his youth, in the years after it was decimated by World War One and the anti-Jewish violence that accompanied it. He finds a nightmarish landscape full of amputated limbs and the ghosts of the town's once-vibrant religious life; on the eve of his return to Palestine he is force to admit that his efforts to rekindle a spark of spirituality have come to nothing.

Each of these is a recognizably different modality of dealing with the ancestral world, entailing a particular kind of narrative framework.

Without delving into their complex motives and strategies, it is enough to point out that in the last two decades of Agnon's life none of them any longer served his purposes. The finality of the destruction of Buczacz in the Holocaust changed the status of the town as an imaginative object and required a new approach. Moreover, Agnon's awareness of his own mortality and of the valedictory nature of the opportunity that lay before him lent urgency to the search for a large project that would stand as a final statement of his relationship to Buczacz and what it represented. That project would have to be novellike in its epic ambitions yet remain loyal to the traditional flexibility embodied in the story as an unapologetic vehicle whose value inheres in itself. The result of that search was *'Ir umelo'ah*.

HAMASHAL VEHANIMSHAL
[THE PARABLE AND ITS LESSON]

The story *Hamashal vehanimshal* is an excellent example of the tensions that generate Agnon's best work in *'Ir umelo'ah*.[13] The story takes place within two time frames. The present time of the story is set around the year 1710 and concerns an elderly shamash, a synagogue sexton, who is put on trial for an act of public humiliation. The tale he tells in his defense, which takes up three quarters of the whole story, is set a half century earlier during the years in which Galician Jewry was recovering from the massacres of 1648. That tale relates how he and Rabbi Moshe, the rabbi of Buczacz, undertake a descent into Gehinnom in order to ascertain the death of a young husband who has abandoned an even younger bride. While in the Netherworld, the shamash discovers a gruesome sight that subverts all his received notions about postmortem rewards and punishments. He sees great Talmud scholars suffering in Hell for the seemingly trivial infraction of talking during the reading of the Torah in the synagogue. It is the grave theological import of this ostensibly minor sin that becomes the subject of a great memorial discourse the rabbi delivers on their return. The Jews of Buczacz are stunned and moved to repentance when they hear this account from the shamash fifty-four years later, and as a sign of its importance the story is inscribed in the communal register. When the ledger is destroyed in the Holocaust, the narrator takes it upon himself to retell the story.

Despite the vast differences between modern readers and the townspeople of Buczacz three hundred years ago, it is fair to say that we are, like them, riveted by the shamash's tale. We are moved to horror and pity by the plight of Aaron, the young scholar encountered in Hell whose efforts to solve the problem of theodicy leads him to an early and alien grave. And even if we no longer believe in a fire-and-brimstone conception of the afterlife, we, like the shamash, cannot help being disturbed by the grotesque punishments of the learned elite in Gehinnom. Most of all, we marvel at the figure of the shamash himself, his laconic loyalty to his master, his obdurate courage in exposing himself to danger, and the intriguing mixture of his motives as he withholds and releases information.

Yet despite these manifold sources of fascination, *Hamashal vehanimshal* remains a problem story in several crucial respects. There is a critical plot line that is left dangling: the rabbi and shamash undertake their perilous visit to Gehinnom for the purpose of enabling a teenage wife to remarry. Yet although they are successful in confirming her husband's death, their errand has no effect on the girl's plight, which is quickly moved to the margins of the story. Moreover, after the sensational revelations about the true nature of Hell, the shamash's tale concludes with a moment-by-moment, word-for-word transcription of the memorial ceremonies on the twentieth of Sivan, the fast day that commemorated the martyrs of 1648, without our being shown the relevance of this lengthy bloc of exposition to themes of the story. Finally, the happy ending is likely to be felt by modern readers to be too happy. This instantaneous, concerted and corporate act of repentance seems too easily purchased and remains at odds with the grimmer vision of human nature presented earlier in the story. Problematic also are the digressions that litter the narrations of both the shamash and the story's overall narrator. Despite the ideal of restraint in speech embodied by the rabbi and advocated at every turn by the shamash, the story cannot be told without frequently yielding to the temptation to explore narrative byways of little patent relevance that dissipate rather than focus the energies of the plot.

Are these issues a sign of Agnon's wavering artistic control in the late stage of his career as a writer? Did he think that presenting tales about Buczacz required less writerly rigor than the existential parables of his middle period? Or did he perceive himself as imitating a pre-modern poetics that did not make the criterion of aesthetic success the taut fitting together of all of the pieces of the story's puzzle? My answer to all these questions is no, and my aim in the following pages is to demonstrate through an analysis of *Hamashal vehanimshal* that what the Torah says of Moses in the final chapter of Deuteronomy can be said of Agnon in his late phase: "His eyes were undimmed and his vigor unabated" (34:7). My argument is based on the assumption that as modern readers we are trained to look for submerged tensions in a text in order to makes sense of its manifest difficulties, and that Agnon relies on this faculty when he puts before us stories told by ostensibly naïve narrators.

In *Hamashal vehanimshal* the tension is between an explicit moralizing theme regarding forbidden speech and a subversive, implicit theme that registers the traumatic effects of both the 1648 massacres and the horrors of Gehinnom. The first theme focuses on the temptation to converse during worship and the reading of the Torah in the synagogue, which are shown to be grave violations with horrific consequences beyond the normal imagining of the townspeople of Buczacz. Even beyond this dramatic but restricted sense, the theme of proper and improper speech resonates at every level of the story: in the communication between the rabbi and the shamash, in the need of scholars to hawk their insights, in the circulation of opinion within the town, in the parabolic form of the great memorial homily the rabbi delivers and, most of all, in the unremitting anxieties of both narrators about exerting their control over their own discourses. On all these levels, the narrators propound an ethics of self-restraint that views all unnecessary speech as a source of bedevilment. Even the most learned and pious are tempted to muffle God's speech—as recorded in the Torah—by the proliferation of their own.

Yet behind and beneath this moralizing message lie darker forces that harbor much deconstructive potential and shape the way the story is told at every turn. The sights the shamash saw as a young man on his visit to the Netherworld were so profoundly disturbing that it has taken him more than half a century to be able to tell the story, even if it has meant depriving the community all the while of the lesson it teaches. Even once the point has been taken, there remains a festering dread about the un-knowableness of actions and their potentially horrendous consequences. That some of the greatest sages of history are suffering the tortures of hell because of what seemed to be merely an excess of zeal is a destabiliz-ing discovery that produces troubling questions about the proportional-ity of human conduct and divine punishment. An even more grievous theological wound is opened up by the Khmelnitski massacres of 1648, which continue to emit waves of destructive energy long after the Jews of Buczacz have reestablished communal life and rabbinic authority. There is barely a page of the story on which these losses are not felt. The very spring for the audacious journey to Hell concerns the rabbi's brilliant student Aaron, who suffers for eternity there because he could not un-derstand how God could let His people be viciously slaughtered.

It is the pressure exerted by the trauma narrative on the narrators' moralizing enterprise that accounts for, I would argue, much of what is strange, discontinuous and unresolved in the story. The digressions remain digressions, but the motives for them become clearer when we understand them as expressions of the narrators' anxieties. The narrators' reliability is undermined by forces they cannot govern. Written on these two levels, *Hamashal vehanimshal* is a story riven by unquiet tensions whose complexity is ultimately in the firm executive control of its author.

A SCANDAL IN BUCZACZ

The eyes through which we see all this are those of the shamash. Un-like the gabbai, a householder who volunteers to distribute roles in the service ("honors") and collect payment for them, the shamash is a wage earner employed by the community. It is therefore precisely because of the office's subservient status that it is an unusual move to place one of its occupants at center stage. After introducing the shamash and describing the story's precipitating incident, the busy and authoritative narrator of *'Ir umelo'ah* steps aside and hands over the narrative to the voice of the shamash and, with a few exceptions, does not repossess the telling of the story until its final section. This is a renunciation of the narrator's executive management. Far from being a marionette, the shamash emerges as his own man: an idiosyncratic mixture of curmudgeonly stubbornness, fiercely reverential loyalty and surprising religious learning. He has a name and a family story, and a fixed location in history, unlike the narrator, who must remain impersonal and anonymous and floating in time. Furthermore, the shamash possesses a special kind of authority. Although the narrator of *'Ir umelo'ah* brandishes the chronicler's near-omniscient overview of the affairs of Buczacz, it was not he who accompanies Rabbi Moshe on this tour of the Netherworld. There is no substitute for hearing about those searing sights directly from the eyewitness.

The handover of the narrative from the narrator to the shamash takes place as a result of the events described in Chapter 1. The unusual occurrence that warrants description is a disciplinary hearing in which a venerable shamash is being accused of the sin of public embarrassment. The violation takes place during Sabbath morning prayers when the shamash notices a young man, the son-in-law of one of the town's wealthiest citizens, speaking to his neighbor during the reading of the Torah; failing repeatedly to get the young man's attention by various eye signals and hand gestures, the shamash descends the bimah, takes the young man by the elbow and escorts him out of the synagogue. All Buczacz is in an uproar over this unprecedented act of public shaming, and the next day the shamash is brought up on charges.

The inherent sensationalism of this precipitating incident is deliberately squandered by the narrator by interrupting it in the middle with a sizable digression concerning the changing customs surrounding the Torah reading in Buczacz. Once upon a time in Buczacz—the time in which the shamash's story is set—the blessing recited by the seven men called to the Torah on Sabbath mornings was a fleeting pause in the public recitation of God's word. By increments over time, this pause was expanded and filled by verbiage of various kinds that distracted the congregation from the reading and even promoted envy and conflict. The narrator is constrained to dissipate the drama and insert the digression because he knows that without it his readers will have little chance of properly construing the shamash's action. His readers—as opposed to the shamash's listeners—live in modern times in which the Torah reading as a circus of honors and announcements has become common practice. The narrator therefore has to work to bridge the distance between reality as we know it and the very different norm that was observed by the holy community of Buczacz at an earlier time in its history. Yet in no sense is this merely an ethnographic footnote. For both the narrator and the shamash, in their respective narrations, success is wholly measured by the ability to restore the credibility of the earlier, purer standard and make people believe that, rather than being a matter of religious nicety, competing with God's word during the recitation of His Torah is, especially for the learned elite, literally a matter of life and death.

The court scene introduces some of the story's key themes: the prerogatives of class, the above-the-law status of scholars, the conflict between eyewitness knowledge and received truths. The narrator is again on hand to explain to us what is so truly provocative in the shamash's behavior as to warrant the formation of an ad hoc beit din and the slapping of an aged community functionary with a fine for enforcing synagogue decorum. Ironically, the reasons turn out to have little to do with the legal principles that ostensibly serve as the basis for the court's deliberations. Public shaming, to be sure, is a matter to which legal culpability attaches in Jewish law. But the narrator does not present it as such; rather, he frames it in terms of a scandalous transgression of social norms. The heart of the matter is the public refusal of a poor person to acknowledge the honor due to two classes, the wealthy and the learned. The strength of the community is sustained by the intertwining of these two classes; distinguished young scholars are taken as husbands for the daughters of successful merchants in a distinctly Jewish version of the process of natural selection. The young man the shamash escorts out of the synagogue is just such a case. The seriousness of *his* infraction is presumably mitigated by two facts. He is not a native of Buczacz, having been recently brought there by marriage, and therefore does not appreciate the rigorousness with which the town treats the ban on speaking during the Torah reading. Moreover, he was uttering words of Torah relevant to the moment at hand—a novel insight into the weekly portion—rather than idle chatter. He is an errant young prince of the law who has been brutally importuned by an impoverished synagogue functionary.

In the face of the amassed authority of the community and its rabbinic judges, this lowly sexton asserts the authority not of what he has learned but of what he has *seen*. When he declares that the humiliation he has visited upon the young scholar is nothing compared to the punishments in the World to Come, he makes his claim based on what his eyes have witnessed. The judge picks up on the peculiarity of this assertion, and, although he stipulates the gravity of the infraction, he pushes the shamash to specify how it is that he has seen things that others, endowed with the same faculty of sight, have not. "The books may offer their condemnations," the shamash insists enigmatically, "but it is the eyes that see what it is to suffer God's wrath" (4). Beneath this verbal sparring lies a profound epistemological provocation. The shamash is asserting that, when it comes to wisdom and truth, what he has seen with his own eyes trumps the official determinations arrived at through textual interpretation and halakhic decision making. This is an assertion that will be both amplified and tested in the course of the story. For example, by finding Aaron in Gehinnom, Rabbi Moshe and the shamash succeed in the object of the journey: they confirm the fact of his death. This is a tragic, heart-rending meeting, yet the knowledge it yields regarding the husband's death has no halakhic standing whatever, despite all the rabbi's efforts to effect the girl's release from the bonds of being an agunah. The evidence of the eyes, whether it is traumatic as in the case of the shocking scenes of suffering or ennobling as in the case of the shamash's veneration of his master, possesses an urgent truthfulness that often eludes the institutionalized orders of meaning and registers fully only in what the reader is privileged to be shown.

Finally, the encounter between the shamash and his examiners adumbrates the theme of silence and its voluntary and involuntary violations. The course of the questioning is worth looking at with some care. The shamash enters the interview with a seemingly unshakable intention of accepting his punishment without explaining himself. But this resolve is soon assailed by unbidden forces within him. "He raised his eyes and shut them like someone who sees something and is terrified by it," the narrator tells us; and he then goes on to explain that just those terrifying sights are the ones that will be related in the tale to follow, and it is those terrors that have now "returned, reawakened and begun to reappear before him" (5). The judge himself sees "all manner of horror etched on his face," and urges the shamash to speak. The shamash rebuffs him and, with a mixture of dignity and desperation, pronounces that he has struggled his whole life to prevent himself from engaging in unnecessary speech, and on this occasion too he will remain true to that principle, whatever the costs. Yet all it takes is for the judge to say perceptively, "I think you *wished* to say something," for the shamash to do an about-face and begin speaking.

> Consternation took hold of the shamash. He raised his eyes to those who sat in judgment of him and began to speak: "It is not because I seek acquittal from this earthly court or because I want to curry favor with the esteemed members of the congregation that I permit my tongue to reveal a profound mystery. I speak so that you may all come to know the true punishment for something that everyone takes much too lightly."

It is evident to the reader that the explicit rationalization given by the shamash for his capitulation—public warning and education—is a fig leaf covering an ungovernable storm of emotion. The truth is that the incident in the synagogue has unhinged his hard-won and long-enduring composure by stirring up a traumatic experience repressed for many decades. The violation of principle is all the more momentous because the matters to be revealed are not ordinary scandals but nothing less than secrets about the fundamental questions of the universe.

Thus we are introduced to a central paradox of the story. On the one hand, the narrators of the story waste no chance to condemn forbidden or unnecessary speech and to adduce evidence of the mortifying consequences of laxity in these matters. Their admonition begins within the restricted purview of the synagogue but extends outward to the marketplace and to the domestic space of family life. It goes so far as to take on the features of an overarching ethical-ontological principle that identifies God's words as the only true speech and human words as a kind of fallen or corrupted speech that, though necessary, should be kept to a minimum. Talking during the Torah reading, which at first presents itself as merely an instance of inconsiderate behavior, thus looms large as the site of a cosmic, catastrophic violation: the aggression of human speech upon the divine word.

On the other hand, there is the evidence of the story itself. This long and unwieldy tale, told by the shamash and staged by the narrator, constitutes in many respects an enormous and flagrant transgression against the very ideal of verbal abstinence that they themselves have so vehemently been promulgating. This wayward prolixity is far from obligatory. To get the business done of describing the horrible punishments of the sinning scholars and thus acquit himself of delivering his monitory message, the shamash could have vastly reduced the amplitude of his account. A principle of utility would have eliminated not only the numerous digressions but also a great swath of the story devoted to describing the conduct of his master, Rabbi Moshe. Yet the reader knows that these seemingly unnecessary accretions and dilations are in fact true expressions of what is really on the shamash's mind: the trauma induced by what he saw so many years ago, and the loss of his connection to the great and holy man he served so devotedly.

OUR MASTER

Why does Agnon's narrator loosen the reins and allow the shamash to take over the story? To be sure, the principled audacity he displays in banishing the talkative young scholar and then standing up to the judges of the rabbinic court marks him as a person of high resolve. But his true merit lies less in his character than in his utility to the story. This is a story about occurrences so remarkable and bizarre that only the authority of an eyewitness account has a chance of overcoming the reader's incredulity. It is a story, moreover, whose principle actor is a taciturn rabbi whose enigmatic actions require careful observation and explication. Who better to observe and explicate them than his devoted personal assistant? The shamash functions as a lens through which we take in the moral and spiritual eminence of the figure referred to, throughout the original text, as *rabeinu*, our Master, as if in using the first person plural the shamash speaks for the community as a whole. As the name of his office implies, the shamash's function is to serve his master. Yet, ironically as we shall see, despite this subservience the gruff and protective secretiveness that surrounds the shamash projects a fascination on the reader that rivals the rabbi's mystique.

It is the rabbi who is placed squarely at the moral center of the story, even if the narrator unintentionally accepts the existence of competing currents of interest. That a moral center be established is crucial to Agnon here, as it is generally in *'Ir umelo'ah*, because the deviations from the norm, which interest his fiction as much as does the norm itself, can be located and described only in reference to the norm. Rabbi Moshe unambiguously occupies that center. He does so not only because of his personal qualities but also because he exemplifies the rabbinic "rulers" of Buczacz. In introducing Rabbi Moshe in the opening sentence of our story, the narrator states that the tale is part of his project "to describe our masters who reigned [*shemalkhu*] one after the other over our town." The succession of Buczacz's rabbis resembles a king list in an ancient chronicle. The rabbi is a Judaic version of Plato's philosopher-king, and in the ideal vision of Buczacz as a *qehilah qedoshah*, a holy community informed by Jewish law, the rabbi, as the *av beit din*, the head—literally, the father—of the court is the ultimate arbiter of authority. Again, it is important to distinguish between the ideal and the idealized. The ruler-ship of the rabbi as an ideal obtains only when, as a class, rabbinic authority is recognized as paramount, and when, as an individual, the rabbi is the worthy exemplar of this high authority.

Already in our story we are witness to a falling away from the ideal; for in the fifty-four years that separate the main events from the present of the telling there is a recognizable diminution of this high standard. A small detail hints at a broad and troubling problem. When it comes to putting together a panel of judges to take up the case of the shamash the day after the incident in the synagogue, the chief rabbi, the town's *av beit din*, recuses himself from the proceedings, explaining that his fondness for scholars may not enable him to give the case of the shamash a fair hearing. Although this compunction presents itself as merely a zealous regard for the honor of Torah study, it is in fact symptomatic of a pervasive and systemic perversion that has infected the religious life of Buczacz. Torah study has become commodified and fetishized, and scholarship has become an arena for performance rather than piety. As presented by the narrator at the outset of the story, the offending son-in-law—and by extension his father-in-law, who "acquired" him for his daughter—are the embodiment of the problem.

> A wealthy man from the upper crust of our town took as his son-in-law a learned young man from a prominent family. The boy was skilled at advancing all kinds of novel interpretations of our holy texts, even when their meanings were already transparent. In fact, sometimes, in his encounter with a text, he would pronounce his own interpretation before he had even digested its plain sense.[14] I refer here not to the nature of his insights but to the fact that his eagerness to propose them overrode any capacity he had for self-restraint. (2)

The ability to come up with novel interpretations (*lehadesh hidushim*) is an index of scholarly brilliance, but when that ability becomes a socially sanctioned compulsion, then brilliance and piety part company. The language produced by human ingenuity competes with the language of the holy texts rather than serving it. If this were simply the young man's particular pathology, then the matter would not be troubling. But he has been "taken" by one of the town's wealthy men precisely because his scholarly brilliance can so readily and abundantly be put on display. The public performance of brilliance has become a valuable commodity for conspicuous consumption.

The craving for ḥidushim and the impatience with the plain meaning of the text are ills that have only recently taken root in Buczacz. This is a town in which respect for God's word is the norm during the Torah reading, and the son-in-law's flouting of that discipline is explained in part by his being an outsider and a recent arrival. Nevertheless, there is growing indulgence for behavior of this kind; tellingly, the wrath of the town is incited not by his transgression but by the shamash's disregard for the respect due the wealthy and the learned. The shamash's scandalous intervention is the gesture that creates a bridge to the Buczacz of a half century earlier when such a permissive and inadvertent collusion would have been unthinkable. This was the era when "Buczacz was Buczacz" and the town was "ruled" by Rabbi Moshe and by the true values he both represented and enforced.

Rabbi Moshe's greatness is established in part by his prophetic ability to identify this tendency to unrestrained performative speech as a sin and foresee that it would bedevil his community long after his death. When he made conversing during the Torah reading the subject of the great discourse he delivered on the twentieth of Sivan, the crescendo of the story and his valedictory address before his death, his listeners must surely have been dumbfounded as to the choice of topic. The rabbi admits that this is a transgression he himself has never witnessed but merely heard about (47). It is only we the readers, who have been given access by the shamash to the dark revelations of Gehinnom, who are positioned to appreciate the momentousness of the rabbi's subject. Yet, like the desperate efforts of his biblical namesake, Rabbi Moshe's fierce homiletic warnings prove incapable of staving off the folly that will take root in the next generation. In the comedic turn the story takes in its conclusion, it is only the courageous ire of the ancient shamash that can break the cycle and prevent the insidious growth from spreading.

There are two other dimensions of the rabbi's character that fill out the norm he embodies: the style of his own learning and his solicitude for Zlateh, the child who is the sole survivor among his relatives of the massacres of 1648. It goes without saying that the rabbi is a great scholar, but it is the particular manner of his greatness that makes a vital connection to the thematic axis of the story. The resources for scholarship, the shamash observes at many points, were greatly different fifty-four years ago than they are in the present of the story. When it comes to books—the term applies only to *sefarim* in the sense of scriptural and talmudic texts and their commentaries—the average householder in Buczacz at the time the shamash tells his story has more books on the shelves of his home than were to be found in the town as a whole at the time of Rabbi Moshe (52). Books were scarce and expensive. The first printed Hebrew books appeared only in the second half of the fifteenth century, and the widespread upheavals caused by the massacres of 1648 disrupted the chain of scholarly transmission and made books even scarcer. In an aside, the shamash relates the story of an important rabbi of the time who was about to die; although he regretted leaving the world, he was consoled by the fact that in the Supernal Academy he would have the opportunity of seeing Tractate 'Eruvin, a major section of the Talmud, which he had never before been privileged to hold in his hands (52). Another anecdote tells of a pair of Talmud students who walk for two days straight because they heard that someone in a neighboring town possessed a copy of the minor tractates of the Talmud. Rabbi Akiva Shas, one of the elders of Buczacz, received his name from the fact that he was the only person in the town to own a complete set of the Talmud (*shas* is an acronym for *shishah sedarim*, the six orders of the Mishnah on which the Talmud forms a commentary, 16). Rabbi Moshe himself has to send to Rabbi Akiva Shas when he needs to consult Tractate Zevaḥim. We are

further informed that in those days, except for the Tanhuma, the texts of
the midrashim were also not available.

Rabbi Moshe's own teacher, the revered Rabbi Mikhl of Nemirov,
was among the slaughtered in 1648. It was as a young man in his academy in Nemirov that Rabbi Moshe was formed as a scholar, and his recall
of those printed texts has had to stand by him after the calamity, when
those texts are no longer available. When the rabbi traces the develop-
ment of prayer as an institution in Bible and Talmud in his great discourse on the twentieth of Sivan, each statement is accompanied by an
exact quotation of the source reference. Which is of course as it should
be, except for the fact that the rabbi has not been privileged to have access to most of these texts since he was a youth studying in Nemirov and
recites them by heart. Although this is assuredly evidence of extraordinary precocity and mental gifts, the true source of the shamash's veneration lies in the rabbi's relationship to the texts he so readily brings to his
lips. In their eagerness to parade their virtuosity, the scholars of today
use passages from Scripture and rabbinic literature as grist for their mill,
as means of reinforcing and showcasing their ḥidushim, those novel interpretations or stunning solutions to textual difficulties by which they
make their mark on the world. Rabbi Moshe, by contrast, places as his
chief object his audience's understanding of the verses from Scripture
rather than the interpretations and constructions built on them. He does
so out of the conviction that, understood correctly, the plain meaning of
the verse speaks for itself. For that reason he enunciates and even chants
each verse, explicating as he goes, so that every member of his flock "can
receive it according to his capacity" (49).[15]

The rabbi's everyday practice provides a model for the proper relation
between human speech and divine speech. This means, first and foremost,
that he says little and speaks only when necessary. His preferred mode of
communication with the shamash is the nonverbal gesture, which is sufficient to convey his meaning; often these are instances in which looking substitutes for speaking. When he does speak, he prefers to make his
points through quotations from Scripture, and when he does quote, he is

careful to insert a brief pause between the quotation and his own words in order to recognize the distinction of one from the other. Rather than giving discursive addresses, his public homilies are strings of verses tied together in thematic strands. In doing so he is not hiding behind the verses or avoiding making his own conceptual formulations; rather, again, he is honoring divine speech and declining to impose his own.

Perplexingly, after delivering these great discourses with their abundance of verses, the rabbi is observed to be in a state of dejection. The shamash reports:

> I have heard two reasons for this. One is that he grew sad after every sermon, because, being a great preacher, he was worried that the beauty of his words overshadowed the message he was imparting. The other is that he worried lest he had said something that was not for the sake of Heaven. Years later, after I had remarried, and Zlateh, may she rest in peace, was my wife, I heard from her that after every sermon he delivered, our Master took upon himself a full-day fast of silence. (58)

The shamash's informant on these matters is none other than Zlateh, the rabbi's young relation on whose behalf he undertook his journey to Gehinnom. (It is only from this casual aside, by the way, that the reader discovers a small trove of background information: that after she was released from her state of being an agunah, Zlateh married the shamash following the death of his own wife, and that Zlateh has died in the meantime.) Both explanations for the rabbi's post-sermon tristesse are connected to the extreme anxiety and even danger inherent in handling divine speech and mixing it with human speech. Handling such materials, so the rabbi's scrupulousness leads him to feel, must inevitably bring with it some culpability; and so the rabbi submits himself to a daylong regimen of silence. *Ta'anit dibur* was not an ascetic practice known from earlier Jewish sources or familiar to European Jewry, and so the shamash permits himself a digression in which he explains how he learned of the practice from one Rabbi Hezkiah, a Buczacz native whose ancestors emigrated from Syria and Babylonia.

It is solicitude for Zlateh, finally, that completes the picture of the rabbi as the embodiment of the norm anchoring the world of the story. Zlateh is the granddaughter of Rabbi Naftali, a relation of Rabbi Moshe and a wealthy wine merchant with dealings with the Polish gentry who used his position to better the political situation of his Jewish brethren. Instead of paying what he owed for a wine shipment, one of those Polish noblemen set his dogs on Rabbi Naftali and murdered him. Shortly after that, all the members of the extended family, except for Zlateh, were slaughtered in the massacres of 1648 or died of sickness or starvation in their aftermath. Surviving as a nearly feral child, Zlateh traveled from town to town with a group of survivors, and when they came to Buczacz, Rabbi Moshe's wife, without at first knowing who she is, arranged for her to be taken into her home. The discovery of her family connection flooded the rabbi, who has suffered so much loss, with a sense of grace and joy. He personally supervises her education and gives her in marriage to Aaron, his prized student. When Aaron inexplicably deserts her, leaving her an agunah at the age of fifteen for the rest of her life, the rabbi is overcome by grief and despondency. But before too long he collects himself and conceives of the idea of visiting Gehinnom. He reasons, correctly it turns out, that Aaron must be dead, because if he were alive it is simply impossible that he would not have sent word to Zlateh and divorced her. The plan to journey to the Netherworld to confirm that fact, it is important to emphasize, is far from being either a swashbuckling adventure or an instance of theological tourism. True, the plan is audacious, but it is also perilous and likely lethal; "visitors" to Gehinnom generally do not return. That the rabbi and the shamash do return is the fact that furnishes the story's sensational premise. Because this dangerous errand lacks probative halakhic value—Zlateh cannot be released from her bonds on the strength of this spectral sighting—the undertaking is an expression of Rabbi Moshe's emotional exigency.[16] Yet rather than diminishing him in our eyes, this knowledge contributes to his centrality in orienting the world of significance the story constructs.

1648

At the opening of the story, after stating his two purposes for telling it (to praise Rabbi Moshe and to warn of the consequences of improper speech), the narrator concludes with a perplexing statement.

> To be sure, some things related here will not square with those who maintain that Buczacz was unaffected by the Khmelnitski pogroms. I leave it to the One who reconciles all matters to settle this one too.

The narrator seems to be engaged in a polemical exchange with unnamed parties who argue that Buczacz was spared in the massacres. Refuting this position is presented as one of the tasks that will be accomplished by the telling of the story, even though it is subsidiary to the narrative's main goals. Invoking God as the arbiter who will finally decide the matter is an equivocal statement. Does it mean that the issue remains vexed despite the story's having been laid out by the narrator? Or does it express confidence in the ultimate—but not public or immediate—vindication of his conviction concerning the town's fortunes during the massacres?

The narrator's antagonist would appear to be none other than the historical record itself. According to most accounts—both contemporary seventeenth-century chronicles and modern historiography—the Jews of Buczacz defended themselves in 1648 and prevented extensive damage to the town, which, because it remained relatively intact, became a refuge for survivors from other destroyed communities.[17] Although the town later suffered damage when it was occupied by Ottoman Turks, in the vast and horrendous spasm of anti-Jewish violence known in Jewish parlance as *gezeirot taḥ vetat*[18] Buczacz was spared. So what then is the proof for the narrator's revisionist assertion to the contrary, an assertion that remains tantalizingly unexplained and requires recondite divine sanction? The proof lies in the anecdotes, incidents and major plot developments that demonstrate the effects of the pogroms at almost every level and at almost every turn in the story. The puzzle is why the narrator chooses not to gather together these abundant instances and adduce them as evidence for an explicit refutation of the assertion that Buczacz eluded the effects of 1648.

There are two related reasons for this disinclination. The story focuses on the spiritual rather than the material or physical damage caused by the massacres. Admittedly, the town was spared overt death and destruction, but the theological crisis provoked by the broad sweep of events, though less stark and exposed, is more profoundly troubling. At the heart of the crisis lies the problem of theodicy: How could the God of Israel have abandoned His beloved people to the blood-thirsty depredations of the gentiles? Within the pious certainties of the shamash, there is ostensibly no crisis: "Because of His love for us, God encumbers us with suffering in order to purge us of the qelipot we have acquired in the lands of the Gentiles and thereby prepare us for the day of His Redemption" (9–10). Yet a multiplicity of evidence, with the case of Aaron's apostasy figuring first and foremost, plays havoc with the neatness of the shamash's explanation. The shamash's own wide-ranging and digressive account of events works to undermine the certainty of his theology. Despite itself, his narrative records how the catastrophe insinuated itself into every aspect of Buczacz life and created a vast reservoir of belated trauma. "Suffering is hard," states the shamash, "hard when it happens and hard afterward" (8). He is referring specifically to Aaron's fate, but his comment on the aftermath of catastrophe radiates throughout the story.

The second reason for the narrator's reticence lies precisely in the anxiety it arouses concerning the gap between the official theology and the suffering that came in the wake of the pogroms, a suffering that has changed shape but hardly diminished. On the one hand, the suffering is there, persisting and ramifying, and no account of life in Buczacz of that time can ignore it. On the other, to name it, to call attention to it as such, would mean to approach closer to the fraught and menacing theological boundary that Aaron has calamitously crossed over. This anxiety is palpable in the shamash's reconstruction of events that took place fifty-four years ago. But does it resonate for the listeners to his tale some two generations later? It is crucial to keep this retrospective time difference in mind. The Buczacz we are introduced to at the opening of the story is a place where a great deal has faded from memory. The community grew and prospered in the second half of the seventeenth century. An accord was reached with the Potocki family, the Polish magnates who owned the town, which granted the Jews residential and occupational equality with Christian residents.[19] There is in evidence more wealth and security and learning. This means not only that the tractates of the Talmud and its commentaries are more commonly available but also that the indiscretion of the scholarly son-in-law of a rich man can be overlooked precisely because he is a scholar and the son-in-law of a rich man.

In the intervening half century, in sum, two things have declined: the effects of the trauma of 1648 and a basic, class-blind piety in which competing with God's word is unthinkable. Which of the two is the true subject of *Hamashal vehanimshal* and the real engine of the shamash tale? It is a question worth asking because both the shamash and the narrator are indefatigable in insisting that the purpose of the story is to underscore the mortal consequences of inappropriate speech. After his lengthy and sensational account of Aaron's apostasy, for example, the shamash is at pains to persuade us that his story is being told only *en passant* as an introduction to the "main thing": "That is the story of Aaron, husband of Zlateh, and it is through his fate that I came to see how severe is the punishment for all who talk during the service and the Torah reading. If this introduction is longer than the story, more severe still is the story itself" (27). The shamash is anxious here and elsewhere to avoid the perception of a symmetry or proportionality between the two themes. And it is not just Aaron's tale that solicits our attention; after the tour of Gehinnom, beginning in Chapter 15 the story turns toward the epic account of the twentieth of Sivan, the communal commemoration of the martyrs who perished in the massacres. Neither theme, in the final analysis, can be left behind. That being the case, we are left to ask a series of questions: Is there a fundamental link between the two themes? Or is this is a story that is burdened with accommodating two separate ideas? And finally, why are the narrators so insistent on foregrounding one over the other? These are questions that will be returned to once the effects of 1648 have been more fully explored.

The damage done by Aaron's apostasy extends beyond the theological questions it raises. By turning Zlateh into an agunah, Aaron's disappearance prevents the fifteen-year-old girl from marrying for the rest of her life. This is a devastating blow to the rabbi because of his affection for her as the lone survivor of his family and his empathic sorrow over the barren life that lies before her. Indeed, he is nearly unhinged by the news. He neglects his communal duties, stops giving his regular public lessons on Maimonides and Alfasi and becomes wholly obsessed with the futile quest for a legal loophole that would release Zlateh from her bonds (10–11). The man who hews to a strict regimen of reticence now finds himself, again futilely, chatting for hours over brandy and cakes with gentile peasants in hope of extracting scraps of information about Aaron's whereabouts. What precipitates this breakdown is not only heartbreak over his poor relative's plight but the disappointment of a broader hope: "Our Master saw in Aaron and Zlateh his aspirations for a new generation that would serve God righteously in place of their parents murdered by the enemy" (8). The rabbi sees in the young couple the seeds of a recovery that would recoup horrendous losses and reestablish the chain of Torah learning. Aaron's desertion therefore signals not just a private sorrow but the prospect of a sliding back into the morass of communal breakdown and disintegration. It is another example of how the trauma of 1648, rather than being contained by the passing years, extends its baleful effects like time-released capsules.

The effort at containment is palpable in the shamash's account of Aaron's fate. The shamash first tells us about the student's religious crisis in Chapter 2, at the point when his disappearance is first discovered, and then again in greater length in Chapter 7, when he is encountered in Gehinnom. In both instances, the affecting and disturbing tale is thickly overlaid with the shamash's stern moralizing. Only when the rabbi and the shamash first come across Aaron's shade is the young man allowed to speak in his own voice. In its mixture of pathos and fatefulness, it is a moment that seems taken directly from Dante's *Inferno*.

> At this Aaron let out a wail and began crying loudly and bitterly. "They never let me! They never let me go to her! They buried me in their cemetery, a Gentile cemetery with a cross on my grave! . . . They cut me off from Jews, and I couldn't even go into a Jewish home. When I wanted to leave my grave to visit my wife in a dream and tell her that I was dead and that she was free to remarry, the cross would bar my way, and I could not get to her. Rebbe, Gehinnom is terrible, but the torment of knowing that I left my wife to be an agunah is much, much worse." (22)

Aaron's remorse comes too late; his responsibility for a grievous wrong cannot be evaded. At the same time, however, he never meant to injure Zlateh, and his own plight is terrible and visited on him for eternity. Yet the shamash is quick to intervene and prevent Aaron from continuing to tell his story in his own words. He explains to his listeners that he will now proceed to narrate Aaron's story in the third person, assuring them that none of the substance of the situation will be lost in converting from one mode to the other (22–23). He further assures the listeners that the shift is merely a technical matter necessitated by the fact he could not retrieve the young man's exact words because of the profound mortification he (the shamash) was experiencing when he heard them.

The shamash's quick appropriation of Aaron's voice answers another need as well. It shuts down the source of pathos that radiates from the young man's situation. Left to tell his own story in his own words, Aaron would reprise and amplify the soul-rending theological emergency that impelled him to take the heedless steps that delivered him to his present fate. The shamash therefore initiates deliberate measures to take over Aaron's story and reframe it in such a way as to minimize the effects of the corrosive doubt consuming the life of the young scholar. He does so by making Aaron's fate into a moral exemplum for the dangers of intellectual inquiry (*ḥaqirah*), which, rather than leading to true knowledge, places the seeker deeper and deeper into the clutches of the *qelipot* (literally, husks), seductive demonic forces that imperil the soul of the believer. This theological schema makes the shamash very much of his time and place and reflects the penetration of Lurianic Kabbalah into the scholarly circles of Polish Jewry, especially through the writings of Rabbi Isaiah Horowitz (c. 1565–1630), the author of the *Shenei luḥot habrit*, which itself was first published in 1648. Aaron is portrayed as a rationalist whose desperate search for reasons for God's apparent abandonment of His people, for which he learns Latin and immerses himself in "alien" wisdom, leads him down a slippery slope to apostasy and death. In that portrayal, the harrowing pathos of Aaron's individual fate, in all its troubling implications, is exchanged for a pitiable case study in a transgression against norms held jointly by the shamash and his pious listeners.

It is worth pausing for a moment to consider how unlikely it would be to find Aaron's story, even as filtered by the shamash, in any text from the period in which our story is set. The explicit wrestling with the problem of theodicy provoked by national catastrophe has a distinctly modern tang to it, as do other features of the story, especially its consciousness of its multiple narrative planes. Indeed, in the final pages of the story, the narrator—that is, the overarching narrator who allows the shamash to recount many of the events—makes direct reference to the Holocaust, in which the communal register recording these events was destroyed. In fact, throughout *'Ir umelo'ah*[20] references to the murder of European Jewry are common, although the events of that period are not represented. This means that Agnon's narrator, in this story as in others, writes about earlier times out of an awareness of what has taken place in his own; and in a profound sense his very motive for telling these stories is fueled by that catastrophic loss. It is therefore not farfetched to say that at some level 1648 is viewed through 1939–1945, and vice versa. 1648 is presented as a kind of rehearsal for the Holocaust, while at the same time the sort of theological crisis Aaron suffers is retrojected from the modern period to seventeenth-century Galicia. The parallel can be taken even further. The Khmelnitski massacres, even though causing vast collective devastation, did not bring about the horrible totality of the Final

Solution. Buczacz survived, albeit in the traumatized state described in our story, and with time Galician Jewry rebuilt its communities and institutions and flourished. Now, this would seem to be where the parallel breaks down, were it not for the fact that there is an offshoot of European Jewry that not only survived but flourished: the Yishuv and the state of Israel. And so there emerges a different kind of parallel, one between Buczacz and Israel. The whole of *'Ir umelo'ah* can be taken as a project in which one is substituted for the other, although it is never wholly clear at any given moment precisely which for which.

As much as *Hamashal vehanimshal* is a story that represents the traumatic persistence of 1648, it is also a story that represents the way in which catastrophe can be mourned. This is not mourning as a state of vanquished dejection but rather mourning as a dynamically active liturgical process that both commemorates the dead and tends to the needs of the living. Agnon devotes a substantial portion of the story to the observance of the twentieth of Sivan; he positions these scenes, especially the rabbi's parables (as in the title of the story), so as to serve as the climax of the narrative, and he makes them thick with quotations from Scripture and the sacred poetry composed to lament the recent disasters. Whether or not the rabbi's parables serve their climactic purpose is a question that will be taken up in a subsequent section. The focus here is on the ceremony of mourning.

Like the ninth of Av, the twentieth of Sivan (a date in the Hebrew calendar that falls in the late spring) is a date to which many calamities have been attached. Its origins perhaps lie in massacres surrounding a blood libel in Blois in 1171 and the day decreed by the Tosafist Rabeinu Tam for its commemoration. Five centuries later, when the Jews of Nemirov were murdered by Cossack bands in the late spring of 1648, the date was taken up in the aftermath as a day of fasting and mourning for all the victims of the massacres, much as in our own time the Warsaw Ghetto Uprising (April 19, twenty-seventh of Nissan) came to stand for the Holocaust as a whole. In the economy of its narrative, *Hamashal vehanimshal* turns away at this point from a preoccupation with the journey to Gehinnom and its aftermath and clears a monumental space for a depiction of the observance of the twentieth of Sivan. Even though the Jewish population of Buczacz is not large—it will become so in the following century—the depiction is monumental in the way it is framed. It is presented as a phenomenon of what might be called liturgical totalization. Every last member of the community, even nursing mothers with their infants, fasts and makes the trip to the cemetery and later stands for hours in the synagogue for the intoning of dirges and the rabbi's eulogy for the dead. There is an intimate, reciprocal relationship between the living and the dead: "Some went to visit their relatives' graves, some to entreat the dead to pray for the living" (39). Even though Buczacz physically escaped the massacres, it has subsequently been turned into a kind of necropolis. The cemetery itself is so overloaded with graves of martyrs that the Rabbi has relocated the venue of the eulogy to the synagogue, lest in the jostling kohanim, Jews of priestly origin, be inadvertently pushed into stepping on burial plots, where they are forbidden to go. For the Rabbi, the omnipresence of the dead is a nightmarish perception rather than an actuality. In explaining the transfer of the ceremony from the cemetery to the synagogue, he says, "Why do I need to go to the dead when they are coming toward me?" (40). The Rabbi's meaning, according to the shamash, is that the town proper contains so many unknown graves of murdered Jews that it may be forbidden for kohanim to reside there altogether. The fact that the Rabbi has not issued a definitive ruling is found curious (*qetsat qasheh*) in the eyes of the shamash, given the Rabbi's usual diligence in getting to the bottom of any legal issue he addresses. We, however, are given to understand that the matter is ultimately not a legal one but the projection of a consciousness enmeshed in the world of the dead.

As the ceremony proceeds, this extended scene comes to focus exclusively on the Rabbi, almost as if, in cinematographic terms, he were the subject of an extreme close-up. The Rabbi, we already well know, is the object of the shamash's veneration, and it is therefore no wonder that his every gesture and utterance is taken to be infinitely meaningful. But the choice to place at the center of the scene a man so wholly absorbed in the reality of the martyred Jews is the sign of a broader narrative strategy intended to expose the depths of the trauma left in the wake of 1648. The Rabbi takes the prerogative of beginning with special memorial prayers for his own teacher, Rabbi Yeḥiel Mikhl of Nemirov, but he soon undergoes a breakdown. He bursts into tears, lays down the Torah scroll and places his head on the scroll. The object of fascination for the shamash and other observers in the congregation is the rabbi's hair. Since receiving a wound to his skull during the massacres, he has not cut his hair, and his face is wreathed with a profusion of silver curls. Rather than attending to the grief that has momentarily disabled him, observers prefer a more transfiguring interpretation.

> After a while he pulled himself up, and his white earlocks shone like polished silver. The interpreters of mystic secrets said that our Master had bathed his head in the waters of grace. His face shone in the crimson glow of the setting sun, but his eyes were closed, and our Master seemed like one who had been on a distant journey. Those same commentators said that he had returned from the far western edge of the world, where the Divine Presence resides, and there he had seen his Master, that holy light Rabbi Mikhl of Nemirov, and all the martyrs with him, sitting in the Academy on High, radiant in the Divine Presence. I do not concern myself with hidden matters—for a person like me what my eyes behold is sufficient—but I agree with those who say that every single one of our Master's curls resembled a silver goblet that has been immersed in pure water. (41)

On the face of things, the kabbalistically attuned observers in the congregation would seem to be merely amplifying the shamash's reverential stance toward the Rabbi. But the mystical ascent they ascribe to him, together with its happy vision of the martyrs basking in God's presence, functions to evade the anguish and bereavement that are the dominant and proper emotions of the moment and the ones that the Rabbi's breakdown truly expresses. Even the shamash, who, with his customary skeptical humility, distances himself from the transfiguring extremes proposed by the mystically inclined, is willing to permit a *resemblance* between the curls and the silver goblet immersed in pure water. The irony is that the Rabbi is indeed momentarily lost in another world, but it is the world of grief, not mystical transport. He recovers and regains control not once but twice, and with his commanding spiritual authority he proceeds to conduct the memorial service, so laden with complex liturgical poems, unflinchingly toward the goal of remembering the dead. The liturgy of that lengthening day, one of the longest days in the calendar, has a number of crescendos, and we shall return to the final parables that give the story its name. Surely one of those heightened moments reflects how the events of 1648 have impressed themselves on his mind: "He recited the names of the towns and villages that had been destroyed, and there was not one town or hamlet that he did not mention, and there was not one community of which he did not enumerate the number of Jews killed in it" (44). It is the tragic, epic and—certainly from the point of view of mental acuity—dazzling recitation of the names of the lost communities that demonstrates not only the abiding vigor of his mind but also the oceanic dimensions of the catastrophe.

GEHINNOM

When it comes to the sensational scenes in the Netherworld, it is important to keep in mind that the shamash's narrative has at least two audiences: within the framework of the story there are the town elders assembled to judge him for his infraction, and outside it there are modern readers reading the story when it first appeared in *Haaretz* in 1958 or when it later appeared as part of *'Ir umelo'ah*. (One can also speak of an ideal *implied* audience created by the expectations of the pious narrator in the act of telling the story; that theoretical construct will be put aside for the present.) The responses of these two audiences to the scenes in Gehinnom are, unsurprisingly, likely to be very different. As modern readers, we have a variety of filters and rubrics through which we might make sense of depictions of grotesque punishments in the afterlife that are foreign to our sensibilities. We can choose to view them as literature rather than theology. When I was required to read Dante's *Divine Comedy* as a freshman in college—the relevance of this particular example will be evident shortly—the poem was presented as a sublime integration of the social, scientific and political ideas of the Renaissance written within the idiom of the contemporary Christian religious imagination. This is an example of just one of the many ways in which we recuperate religiously exotic material by "appreciating" it rather than feeling called on to accept or reject the credal demands it makes on us. We are likely to respond to the Gehinnom scenes in *Hamashal vehanimshal* with a similar mixture of fascination and curiosity. In fact, the more fantastic and grotesque, the greater our fascination and curiosity.

The reaction of the listeners within the story is quite otherwise. They are shaken to the core, as was the shamash fifty-four years ago when he underwent the experience and as he now relives it. They are deeply disturbed because his eyewitness account contradicts essential elements of their beliefs about the afterlife. As Galician Jews living at the end of the seventeenth century, they are profoundly anxious about the fate that awaits them after death, and their absorption in imagining the afterlife, it needs hardly be said, has little to do with literary or anthropological fascination. The learned Jews depicted in the story were living at a time in which there had recently been a dramatic expansion in imagining the fate of the body and soul after death. Historians have long emphasized the fact that a belief in an afterlife became an official part of the religion of the Jews only after the biblical period. The rabbis of the Talmud authorized the existence of a postmortem Gehinnom (Hell) and Gan Eden (Paradise) and promulgated a doctrine of resurrection and tied them together with a belief in a messianic redemption at the end of history. Yet despite their insistence on the credal status of these beliefs, which were made into an integral part of the daily and Sabbath liturgy, the Rabbis discouraged speculation on these matters and provided tantalizingly little concrete information about what would happen in the afterlife. In the Middle Ages, this vacuum was abhorred by some and reaffirmed by others. Maimonides seconded the belief in resurrection, but only after discouraging speculation about it and only with the provision that it is solely the intellect that survives death and not the body. In contrast to this philosophical rationalism, the mystical tradition had no inhibitions about elaborately imagining the workings of the divine mysteries, whether they included the flow of divine energy within the Godhead or the abstruse geography of Hell.

The dissemination of kabbalistic ideas among Polish Jews intensified and broadened remarkably at the beginning of the seventeenth century. Meditation on divine mysteries, centered especially on the text of the Zohar, had long been a secret occupation of individual elite scholars. The theosophical innovations of Isaac Luria and his circle in Safed in the sixteenth century not only created a more applied and activist theology but also took an evangelizing stance toward promulgating that theology far beyond a narrow circle. Through their writings, Moses Cordovero and Isaiah Horowitz (known as the Shelah Hakadosh) restated Luria's ideas in an approachable form and integrated them into familiar genres of ethical and pietistic guides. In this fashion, teachings that had been limited to an esoteric group of Sephardi mystics in the East were transferred to Polish Jews over the course of the seventeenth century and, in more domesticated and exoteric guise, became an essential part of everyday piety. Within this new framework, the religious imagination was liberated when it came to the afterlife, amply filling in the gaps left by the laconic restraint of the sages of the talmudic period. A good place to find these new imaginings about the afterlife gathered together is the *Reishit ḥokhmah*, a widely popular and oft-reprinted compendium of ethical teachings by Elijah de Vidas, a student of Cordovero's, which first appeared in 1579. In chapter 13, de Vidas brings together texts bearing on the afterlife from the Talmud and the Zohar, as well as from Masekhet Gehinnom, a work of unknown provenance.[21]

The picture that emerges in these accounts is various and shifting in its details but never less than gruesomely vivid. There are seven compartments (*medorim*) in Gehinnom containing various kinds of sinners and five kinds of fire. Every compartment is divided into seven thousand holes, and their breadth and height are each three hundred years' journey. Each compartment is presided over by a special angel, who in turn commands thousands of subsidiary angels of destruction. The punishments of Gehinnom are meted out on the principle of an eye for an eye. Slanderers hang by the tongue, robbers by their hands, adulterers by their sexual organs, wanton women by their breasts, and coveters by their eyes. Whereas the Talmud sees Gehinnom as a purgative ordeal lasting twelve months, the medieval accounts fix twelve months as a sentence that must be served in *each* of the compartments, as the suffering soul is lowered from one to the other in a succession of increasingly severe tortures.

In constructing the compartments of Gehinnom that figure so sensationally in *Hamashal vehanimshal*, Agnon had recourse to another important source from a very different cultural sphere. Immanuel of Rome (1261–1328), a contemporary of Dante's, was a satirical Hebrew poet who introduced the sonnet into Hebrew poetry. In his collected poetic works—he called his diwan the *Maḥbarot*—there is an extended cycle in rhymed prose titled "Hatofet veha'eden," which describes a tour of Hell and Heaven guided by the biblical Daniel. Immanuel Judaizes Dante by replacing Christian schemata with the Rabbis' teachings on Gehinnom in the Talmud while preserving the poetic conventions of the *Divine Comedy*. To be sure, the *Maḥbarot* did not circulate widely in rabbinic circles, yet Immanuel's composition was well enough known to be banned by Yosef Karo in the *Shulḥan arukh*. Although it is unlikely that this particular vision of Hell would have been known to the elders of Buczacz listening to the shamash's tale, it was certainly known to Agnon. And even if there are no borrowings from Immanuel in the story's Gehinnom scenes, the reader familiar with the history of Hebrew poetry hears the echoes of Dante in Jewish guise in Agnon's very enterprise of exploring this territory.

In sum, an unprecedented expansion of the Jewish theological imagination in the Middle Ages provided Agnon with much material to draw on in constructing these key scenes in his story. Indeed, the template for each scene is conventional, and therefore familiar, in giving a name to a compartment, specifying its dimensions, citing the angel appointed to supervise it, explaining the nature of the sins being punished and sparing no grisly or horrific detail in the execution of those punishments. Yet if these scenes are conventional in their presentation of the afterlife and familiar from the medieval ethical literature, then why is it that the shamash was so deeply shaken when he saw these sights many years ago, and why are his listeners in the present time of the story similarly shaken? The answer is that although the template is familiar, the content Agnon has placed within it is a radical departure that subverts some of the deepest convictions of the Jews of Buczacz. To understand the disturbing originality of Agnon's account, let us first delineate the four distinct scenes that make up the tour of Gehinnom.

There are altogether four scenes from Gehinnom: (1) Kaf Haqela (the Sling), (2) Tsalmavet (Shadow of Death), (3) Gag 'al Gag (Roof upon Roof), and (4) the Tatar horsemen. (The fourth scene differs from the rest; it has the characteristics of a nightmarish vision particular to the shamash's febrile imagination. When he speaks of his tour of Gehinnom, he does not include it, speaking only of three compartments.) The first contrasts with the second and the third in that it precedes the encounter with Aaron's shade and is in fact a series of tortures that take place *outside* Gehinnom. It is additionally distinct from those two in the confidence with which the shamash explains the scene; he does not need the rabbi to parse the meaning of strange and inscrutable practices. Based on a passage in the Talmud (Shabbat 152b), the scene describes sinners being flung by gigantic slingshots from the gates of Gehinnom back to the original sites of their sins, which, because of their sins, are no longer identifiable. Having failed to enter Gehinnom, they are flung back and forth until they are wholly worn down. Worse than the fate of confirmed sinners is that of those who wanted to sin and had sinful thoughts but lacked the opportunity to sin. Because of lack of commission, they cannot avail themselves of the process of regret and contrition that purges sin; it remains with them forever. Worse still are "those contemptible people who feel false pangs of conscience and fancy that they have repented, yet all the while they are consumed by sinful thoughts and their illusory pleasures" (20). Of these latter, says the shamash not without a note of grim humor, "No one can accuse me of loving sinners, but when I see them flung around like that, I am quite ready to hire myself out as the doorkeeper of Gehinnom so I can personally let them in" (20).

The Kaf Haqel'a scene established disorientation as the sign under which all the subsequent matters relating to Gehinnom will be presented. What happens in the Netherworld, the shamash tells his listeners, does not conform to your notions, and it is much worse than you think. The norms and hierarchies we live by do not apply there. Reason and received rabbinic teaching would dictate that sins actually committed warrant a more severe punishment than those merely contemplated, but not so in *that* world, in which the order is reversed. You would think that the quest of the sinner to return to the site of his sin and expiate it would be rewarded, but the infernal ordeal into which he has been thrust makes that impossible. You would think that Gehinnom is terrible, but in fact there are those for whom admission to Gehinnom would be a kindness. This first iteration remains abstract; the sins of the sinners are not named. The stunning, upending news to come is that there are sufferers in Hell who, remarkably, resemble—and in most cases are superior in learning and scholarship to—the shamash's listeners themselves.

This cognitive disorientation is explicitly named in the descriptions of the second and third compartments. The first is called Tsalmavet [Shadow of Death] and the second Gag 'al Gag [Roof upon Roof]. Both compartments are filled with innumerable scholars, heads of yeshivot and chief rabbis, from the time of the Mishnah through the period of the Spanish Inquisition to the present. In the first, the scholars are floating in space and separated from each other by great distances, and in the second they are piled one atop the other. Central to both is a grotesque scene of desire repeatedly frustrated. The myriad scholars are all puffed up with self-importance, and each believes that the fate of Torah wisdom depends solely on him. And he wants nothing more than to broadcast his novel insights and arguments and induce his fellow to acknowledge his superior acumen. But not only is the wished-for acknowledgment denied, the very possibility of communication is nullified in the most gruesome way. In the first compartment, the ears of the listener grow bigger and bigger until they cover his entire body and muffle the scream that dies in the throat of the scholar who sought to impress him, whose own lips have enlarged to engulf *his* body. In the second compartment, the lips of the speaker fly away from him, and his tongue becomes impaled on his teeth and swells to the size of a church bell. His listener attempts to yell from horror, but no sound comes out of his mouth. "I am an old man and have seen much trouble and travail," says the shamash, "but misery like that I have never seen."

This cognitive disorientation is explicitly named in the second scene, the compartment of Gehinnom called Tsalmavet. "Nothing in the world is as paradoxical [*davar vehipukho*] as that compartment. It is circular in shape but appears square, square in shape but appears circular. The eyes perceive it one way, the mind another. These differences in perspective induce a certain melancholy" (28). The compartment is notable for being neither hot nor cold and totally airless, and for being presided over by a nameless angel who does nothing but stand with his mouth agape "like a person utterly bored and about to yawn." The population of this compartment is huge, "twice the number of people who went out of Egypt," and, as is evident from their accoutrements (silver-collared talitot and large tefillin), they are all heads of yeshivot and chief rabbis of whole regions, and they are all prodigious Torah scholars with total mastery of the Talmud with its earlier and later commentators. What is most unnerving about this scene is how these mighty throngs are situated. Each is separated from the other by a distance of two thousand cubits (a Sabbath boundary), and because their eyes have grown dim from study they cannot see the hundreds of thousands of similar scholars who float in the space surrounding them. Each, literally, is full of himself and, puffing himself up, proclaims, "I'm all alone in the world; all wisdom dies with me" (29). When he finally manages to prop himself up and realizes that the tiny distant creatures are also Jews, his overwhelming desire is to bestow on them some of his *pilpul*. (Pilpul is the intellectual gymnastics employed by advanced scholars to resolve difficult legal problems.) But as soon as he conceives of this plan, he falls into a desultory sleep.

What happens next in the shamash's description of this compartment can only be described as a scene of talmudic jousting that is a parodic enactment of pilpul itself. The sleeper awakes to see someone striding toward him, and the two begin to trade taunts. One claims that he possesses a pilpul greater than anyone else has ever conceived; the other retorts that the first has stolen his words and that *he* possesses a pilpul that the other would long to hear with every fiber in his body. The two now enter into a parody of scholarly etiquette in which each, supposedly deferring to the other, in fact claims the right to speak first. But the contest turns out to be pointless because communication proves impossible. As soon as one begins to speak, his ears expand until they cover his entire body. The two stand facing one another, utterly mortified and wanting to cry out. But the "first one's scream dies in his throat, and the other's is muffled by his ears." The total effect of their panic on the torpor of the presiding angel is to make him rock back and forth; he would have destroyed them if he had not been striving to produce a yawn.

The second compartment, Gag 'al Gag (Roof Upon Roof), described in Chapter 11, visits a similar punishment on its scholarly inhabitants but stresses other aspects of their ordeal. The hugeness of this compartment consists in its spatial dimensions rather than its population. Not only is it so vast that no boundaries are perceptible to the eye but the compartment as a whole is suspended within a void (*talui 'al belimah*). The inhabitants all have prominent foreheads and pinched eyes from excessive study, and they are frozen in an endlessly repeated gesture in which they pluck hairs from their beards and float them into space. Yet instead of being isolated from one another in this vastness, as they were in the other compartment, here they are piled one atop the other. In this crush, they do in death what they did in life: they pronounce ḥidushim. The difference between their scholarly activity now and then results from the peculiar conditions of academic integrity that are involuntarily visited upon them by Gehinnom. When they were alive and going about their business of issuing ḥidushim, if they found they had been hasty or exaggerated and thus made an error, they always had available to them the option of retraction. But here in Gehinnom, every word they uttered while alive is "permanently engraved in public view with his signature attached" with no possibility of denial.

The corruption of Torah study by grandiosity is the sin that has landed these prodigious scholars in Gehinnom. When a scholar penetrates the contextual truth of a passage of Talmud (*poshet lo devarim kifshutam*), the truer his insight the less his need to inflate his importance on the strength of it. But the more forced and over-ingenious is his insight, the more desperate he is to put it on display to his colleagues. And thus his punishment in Gehinnom. When he opens his mouth to broadcast his ḥidush, his lips fly away from him, and when he sticks out his tongue to find his lips, his tongue gets impaled on his incisors and begins to swell. The tongue thickens and swells up to the size of a church bell, a figure of speech the shamash insists is apt, "for just as a church bell peals without knowing why, so the tongue wags without knowing why it was put into motion" (32). The scholar he was seeking to address now tries to cry out in fright, only to have his own scream swallowed between his lips. It is little wonder that the angel appointed over this compartment of Gehinnom is called Otem, after the Hebrew verb that designates the shutting of the ears and the failure of comprehension.

In gauging the panic and horror these sights induce in the shamash, it is important to recall once again the function of dramatic irony in the story. We the readers have been given by the narrator some preparation for inferring a correlation between the particular punishments inflicted on these scholars and the particular sins that provoked them, by means of the remarkable opening scene of the story: the embarrassment of the garrulous son-in-law and his banishment from the synagogue. But the shamash, so many decades earlier, comes upon these tortures entirely unprepared, and when he does react there is a "double whammy" effect to his reaction. He is unhinged at first by the absence of an evident explanation for the tortures he has witnessed; yet once an explanation is provided by the Rabbi, the shamash's panic grows greater instead of being mitigated. The first wave of the shamash's response is horror because the boundary between him and the tortured souls momentarily disappears and he feels that the same grotesque tortures may be happening to him. "Panic seized me. Maybe *my* mouth was contorted. Maybe *my* lips had flown apart" (32). Having hidden his face out of horror in the folds of the Rabbi's cloak, the shamash loses his bearings, and he fears that his ears are growing to enclose his body. When he wordlessly implores the Rabbi for an explanation, it is not delivered immediately. The Rabbi first takes the shamash's measure to determine exactly how much he is capable of understanding, and the shamash uses the benefit of his retrospective wisdom to delay the rush of events and interpolate a vignette about a Jewish jeweler who measured the ears of the Gentile noblewoman so that he could fashion earrings of exactly the right proportions. The Rabbi even makes the shamash ask a second time, for he "wanted to see how important my question was to me. Sometimes the mouth wants to ask more than the heart wants to know" (33). This wisdom about unnecessary speech, which is the moral preoccupation of both the narrator and the shamash throughout the story, is, again, retrospective wisdom that was not available to the shamash when he first gazed upon these hellish afflictions.

When, after several additional delays, Rabbi Moshe fashions his custom-made response, he delivers a series of clarifications that provide some explanation but no consolation. He explains, to begin with, that what they have seen is a special compartment of Gehinnom—a kind of infernal VIP lounge, so to speak—reserved for great rabbis, heads of yeshivot, and rabbis of whole regions. Special emphasis is placed on the fact that these torments have been in operation for ages, and that the pitiable denizens of this compartment include sages from the time of Talmud and the expulsion from Spain. The nature of their punishments, he goes on to point out, are dictated by the nature of their offenses; because they sinned in matters of speech, they are punished by being rendered mute. If in life they sat one atop the other in the synagogue and beit midrash blathering to each other, now in death they are spread out at a great distance from one another and cannot get a word out of their mouths. They are tantalized by being free to produce all the hidushim they wish and at the same time obstructed in communicating them to anyone else. At the root of their reprehensible behavior during their life-time—the fundamental key to all their troubles—was the sin of talking and flogging their hidushim during prayers and the reading of the Torah: "Our Master's words disturbed me more than anything my eyes had seen" (34). When the shamash first came upon the afflicted souls with-out the benefit of any accompanying explanations, the monstrousness of their suffering seized him with raw terror; but that terror had nothing to do with him personally. Now, with the benefit of those explanations, the terror has metamorphosed into a cognitive-theological-moral complex that has turned around to seize him by the throat. "Who can say that he has never committed that sin?" anguishes the shamash. "Who among us keeps his lips and tongue under control at all times? Who has not talked during the service or the Torah reading? And if those learned in Torah bear such a punishment, what about the rest of us?" (34). Although he well knows that conversation during prayers is a transgression, his mind simply cannot stretch itself to comprehend the rationale for an other-worldly retribution so extreme in its ferocity. Using his best scholastic casuistry, the shamash can appreciate the regrettable extra burden placed on the angels, who now have to exert themselves to separate out true prayers from idle conversation. But this consideration does not go very far in addressing the disturbing phenomenon of the incommensurabil-ity between sin and punishment. The shamash glumly concludes, "The matter still remains unsettled" (35).

A surprising digression at this juncture in the narrative makes an important connection between two of the story's preoccupations. The shamash is struggling to resolve the troubling contradiction between a seemingly minor offense and its terrible punishment, when he suddenly halts his story and surveys his listeners, among whom, he realizes, are scholars as well as community leaders who are not scholars. He turns to them and says:

> Now listen to me all you people of Buczacz. You think that Gehinnom is only for Torah scholars. Well, let me tell you otherwise. There is one area there compared to which all the rest of Gehinnom is like Gan Eden. I never noticed it at first because it was covered in dust. But the voices that could be heard through the dust suggested that there were people there. I could not tell if they were people or cattle or fowl until I went in and saw that it was one huge market fair, like the ones our great-grandparents and those who came before them used to tell about, before Khmelnitski, may his name be blotted out. There were traders, dealers, noblemen and noblewomen, goods galore—like you've never seen before. Silver and gold and all kinds of expensive things. Then suddenly the whole fair was thrown into a panic. The Tatars had arrived. They came on swift horses in rumbling hordes. My body trembles even now as I recall it. I will stop talking about it and go back to where I left off. (35)

The shamash's outburst is all the more intriguing for its strangeness and disconnection from what comes before and after it. Although he labels the scene of the fair and the horsemen as yet another compartment (*mador*) of Gehinnom, it quickly becomes recognizable as connected to the Tatar incursions of the 1670s rather than to the afterlife. It is different from anything that has come before because the suffering it represents is unrelated to any misdeeds that might have provoked it, and the ordeal is collective in nature rather than pertaining to the culpability of the individual soul. The scene belongs, in short, to an entirely different kind of discourse: the historical tribulations of Israel in recent persecutions. Even within this category, there is much that remains strange. Rather than picturing recent events, the tableau evokes an imagined earlier era of great commercial wealth and weighty transactions between Polish rulers and Jewish traders at the great market fairs. It is this older world that is made the target of the swift and devastating incursions of the Tatar horsemen, scourges that in fact come from a later period, the

1670s. The conflation of time and the sketchy, fragmentary evocation of events lend this scene the quality of a nightmare. It can be understood as a posttraumatic memory in light of all we have gleaned from the pervasive persistence of 1648 in our story. "My body trembles even now as I recall it," confesses the shamash.

The digression breaks off as abruptly as it began. Yet by the time the shamash regains his composure and determines to "go back to where I left off," he has unwittingly broached the link between the two kinds of trauma in the story, both hitherto presented as unrelated to one another. On the one hand, there are the events of 1648 and their pervasive baleful consequences for all the Jews of Buczacz, including the shamash's wife, who witnessed the murder of her parents and seven siblings (43), and the shamash himself, whose family was also wiped out. The orphaning of Zlateh and the apostasy of Aaron also belong to this line of the narrative. On the other hand, there are the horrific tortures suffered by prideful and self-important scholars in Gehinnom forming the main story the shamash has been relating. Although a connection between them is made neither by the narrator nor by the shamash, they are both alive and comingled in the unconscious imagination of the shamash, as evinced by the digression about the Tatar horsemen and its surprising placement within the tour of Gehinnom. There is of course an implicit connection between the two, but it is one that is not thinkable to the figures in the story—except perhaps Aaron. It is only we, the modern readers, who, through Agnon's agency, can see it clearly. It is the shared theological problem of incommensurability. How is it possible that the sins of Ukrainian Jewry were so unspeakable as to have warranted the horrors of Khmelnitski and his hordes? How is it possible that infractions of well-meaning scholars can result in unspeakable tortures for eternity? In both cases, the physical afflictions are horrible enough in their own right, but the enduring suffering, when it comes to the surviving and living, comes from the festering cognitive-theological wound that has been opened up.

The coexistence and even commingling of 1648 and Gehinnom in the shamash's mind beg further questions: Is one the *result* of the other?

Is the preoccupation with matters beyond the grave an outcome of a consciousness rooted in mass death and sacrifice? Is it the pervasiveness of death, arising from persecutions that took place in a concrete political-historical context, that generates the anxiety about postmortem punishments and their stringencies? The answer to these questions, as well as to the question of incommensurability, are located beyond the theological imagination of both the narrator and the shamash; the farthest they can go is to mark the wall that has been reached with the modest understatement, *qetsat qasheh* (It is a little difficult).[22] The notion that 1648 may be the generating cause is expressed in the shamash's repeated insistence that the tale of Aaron's apostasy and his discovery in Gehinnom is merely preparatory and subservient to the main moral teaching about inappropriate speech. It is ultimately in the narrative syntax of the story that Agnon wrestles with these questions. The shamash returns from his tour of Hell between Yom Kippur and Sukkot, with many questions about the plausibility of what he has witnessed buzzing in his head; but within half a chapter it is suddenly late spring, and the monumental description of the twentieth of Sivan memorial takes over the story. Immersion in the 1648 theme kidnaps the story for the length of these protracted ceremonies, until the point at which the Rabbi at the very end arrives at his parable, which he uses to refocus the narrative and once again underscore the gravity of inappropriate speech. The story as a whole, in sum, stages a contest in which the spiritually wasting forces of death unleashed by 1648 are resisted by the desire to impose a moralizing meaning on the experience of life and death.

Stepping back and looking at the Gehinnom episode as a whole, we see clearly its extraordinary nature. On his return, the shamash himself can barely believe it has taken place because it is so disturbingly at odds with what he knows about the afterlife. Having been plucked from time and space and exposed to confounding horrors, he has difficulty in accommodating to the fact that life in Buczacz proceeds as usual. Perplexingly, the rabbi takes no action on Zlateh's case as a result of having confirmed the fact of Aaron's death. Her situation, in fact, is resolved only when a mysterious emissary from the East comes to Buczacz bearing a writ of divorce, which could only have been written when Aaron was alive. Yet despite these peculiarities, the shamash insists on the truth of his experience: "The three compartments of Gehinnom that I have noted I saw while completely awake and not in a dream. The same goes for the judgments visited upon all who talk during the prayers and the Torah reading" (39). And whatever hesitations the shamash himself may have had, the people of Buczacz are entirely persuaded by his testimony. So much so that they treat him like a revered authority, surrounding him and pestering him with endless trivial questions about the precise conditions that obtain in Gehinnom (Chapter 25).

What then, in the end, is so shocking about the news the shamash brings back from Hell? In light of the widespread diffusion of expanded ideas about Gehinnom among Polish Jews in the seventeenth century, what is revisionary about the shamash's tale, and by extension what is original about Agnon's appropriation of these materials? First the minor discrepancies. There was neither fire nor snow in the compartments that the shamash observed, which is at odds with all written accounts. The Talmud states that there are three entrances to Gehinnom (one in the desert, one in the sea and one in Jerusalem; Eruvin 19a), yet the Rabbi was able to find a portal only a short distance from Buczacz. The Talmud further states that the tortures of Gehinnom last twelve months, yet the shamash observed souls suffering their afflictions, according to the Rabbi, for hundreds and even thousands of years.

And then there are the three major discrepancies. The first is the fact that the Rabbi and the shamash survived their descent into the Netherworld. An extraordinary sage may outfox the Angel of Death and be given the privilege of entering the afterlife directly, that is, without going through the pangs of death and the grave, and even then his destination can only be Paradise and not its alternative. There is also the case of the zaddik who, on his death, descends into Gehinnom for the purpose of helping his followers discharge their purgations, but he does not rejoin the living. (Immanuel of Rome does descend and return alive, but the account of his journey belongs to the more worldly tradition of secular Hebrew poetry that would not have been familiar to the world of Buczacz.) The return of the Rabbi and the shamash to the world of living remains astonishing. The second is the fact that Gehinnom contains great Torah scholars. Attaining the status of a true *talmid ḥakham* entails not only mastering the corpus of talmudic literature and its attendant commentaries but also contributing to the corpus by making innovative interpretations and proposing creative solutions to knotty dialectical problems. In the normative religious culture of Polish Jewry, the *talmid ḥakham* was the crown of Creation, the pinnacle of aspiration. If Gehinnom contains compartments for sages alongside those for common sinners, then an entire structure of value is put in question, with profound implications for a society whose elite is founded on marriage alliances between successful merchants and promising scholars. If scholars, despite their peccadilloes, cannot count on being exempted from the tortures of Hell, then what hope is there for Jews who face the uncertainties of the afterlife without their attainments?

Finally, the doctrine of sin and punishment is founded on the principle of proportionality in two senses. Minor transgressions warrant minor punishments and major transgressions major punishments. The manner of the punishment is fitted to the manner of the transgression (adulterers hanging by their sexual organs, etc.). Agnon's Gehinnom preserves the latter but throws over the former. The story hews ingeniously to the principle of an eye for an eye in inventing infernally apt punishments for those self-important scholars who cannot help hawking their latest wares during the synagogue service. But when it comes to believing that such infractions—and many would see them as merely excesses of holy zeal—deserve eternal torture, it is only the Rabbi who takes this for granted. For everyone else, including the shamash, this new information is a kind of wild card that threatens the integrity of an entire hierarchy of religious meaning with its implicit balances and gradations. True, the people of Buczacz are eventually persuaded by the force of the shamash's tale to accept the radical seriousness of this particular offense. But beneath their burst of moral revivalism lies a deeper anxiety. With the notion of pro-portionality destabilized, they have lost the reliable key to the map of their religious fate. The desperate desire to regain this certainty is most likely the reason behind the zeal the Jews of Buczacz display in eventually embracing the shamash's message. Despite the shockingly extreme pun-ishments meted out for ostensibly moderate transgressions, the essential principle of theological rationality is reaffirmed. They seize a chance to gain hold of a key that will make sense of their postmortem fate even if they are required to hold themselves to a new moral standard.

THE SHAMASH'S TALE

Within the larger narrative galaxy of *'Ir umelo'ah*, Agnon's postwar sto-ries of Buczacz, our story stands out because it boasts two narrators.[23] One is the narrator who organizes, accompanies and relates most of the volume's stories. The other, of course, is the shamash, to whom the general narrator hands off the story in Chapter 2 and from whom he takes it back in Chapter 24, with a number of intervening glosses and explanations. In allowing the shamash to tell so much of the story, the narrator is discharging his role as an impresario of memory rather than simply as a chronicler. He is for a time divesting himself of his implicit prerogative as master storyteller and welcoming, as it were, a guest artist to share the podium. The gifts brought by this visiting performer are evident. He is a direct participant in the events and can speak with the immediacy of an eyewitness. But does not the narrator of *'Ir umelo'ah* claim for himself a trans-historical omniscience that would give him all the knowledge he needs to tell the story of the shamash and rabbi himself? His knowledge, after all, goes forward in time as well as back-ward, and it is only he who can make reference to the Holocaust at the end of the story and explain that the present iteration of the story is a replacement for the account inscribed in the communal register, the pinqas, which burned in the destruction of Buczacz by the Nazis. What he *cannot* do, however, is embody himself as a historical character with a name, a wife—two wives, in fact—and a real-life role to play in the life of the town. Embodiment is the one thing that the narrator, with all his "super powers," cannot attain.

Yet despite this vital difference, there remains a great deal that the narrator and the shamash share. Their religious outlooks are similar in their worldly piety and their devotion to the core norms of worship and Torah study. They both repeatedly insist on the fidelity of their reporting and on the scrupulous honesty with which they admit what they know and what they do not know. And they both have a pronounced penchant for digressions and the rationales that seek to justify them. Indeed, it is not easy to pry apart the texture and timbre of their individual narrative voices; and this affinity gives rise to an anxiety on the narrator's part concerning the reader's ability to keep the two separate. At the beginning of Chapter 7, when the shamash is in the midst of recounting the tale of Aaron's apostasy and its grim consequences, the narrator feels compelled to intervene and address the reader directly.

> I remove myself from the narrative and take on the character of the shamash so he can speak in his own voice. But lest you start thinking that this story is about me, I intrude periodically with the words "the shamash said." (21)

The Hebrew beneath this idiomatic rendering describes a rather complex act of self-negation and appropriation. The Hebrew reads: *mafshit ani et tsurati velovesh et tsurato shel hashamash venotel et leshono befi* ("I dematerialize my own form and take on the form of the shamash and take his tongue into my mouth"). On the one hand, the narrator wants the reader to know that the story is not about him but about the shamash, even though they are both using the first person. He therefore proposes a device for eliminating confusion and marking the shamash's speeches: he will insert the words "Thus said the shamash." On the other, he insists that the reader understand that, even though the shamash was a real person who toured Hell in the seventeenth century, *in this belated telling* he is a device, a character created by the narrator whose very voice is produced by an act of ventriloquism. The narrator's anxiety, in the end, is not for nothing. He succeeds so well in making the shamash an indelible character that we often forget who in fact is pulling the strings.

Who is the shamash, after all, that this extraordinary tale should be placed in his mouth? By what merit is he allowed to return from Gehinnom alive and tell a story that changes the lives of his fellow townspeople? The elders of Buczacz, having assembled to judge him and now in thrall to his account, ask the same question. Between the description of one compartment of Gehinnom and the other, they wonder:

> You might think that this was because he was great in Torah and wisdom and piety and good deeds. Not at all. This was a poor shamash, one who was no different from anyone else in Buczacz, except for his temper. Perhaps the merits of his forebears who were killed in the pogroms stood in his stead. But in this matter he was no more privileged than the other townspeople, almost all of whom saw their father or mother die a terrible and cruel death. So the matter is truly puzzling. (30)

The shamash himself would make no exception to this characterization. He goes out of his way to underscore his ordinariness in relation to the learned elite of Buczacz. In commenting on mystical speculations relating to why Rabbi Moshe's life was spared during the massacres, the shamash professes that such matters are beyond him: "It is enough for a man like me to get through the weekly portion with Targum and Rashi's commentary" (6). He is, moreover, a man burdened with sorrows. He was a young man with many children at the time of the journey to Gehinnom; his wife was already an invalid, bedridden and unable to speak, who would not live out the year.

Yet despite his lack of distinction, the shamash leverages prodigious power on the people of Buczacz. His power derives not so much from the fact of his journey to Gehinnom as from the telling of it many years later. In the galaxy of Agnon's fiction, storytelling is an omnipresent and highly privileged activity, but rare indeed is the case when the telling of a story has the impact described in *Hamashal vehanimshal*. When his listeners reach the point at which they are too terrified by his story to press for more details, the shamash drives home his advantage: "But he did not leave it at that and proceeded to tell the story to its end, and his words sank deep into their bones and stayed with them all their days. And when they passed away, they saw in another world everything the shamash had told them in this one" (45). What is the source of this power, so rare among great preachers and scholars but here invested in a curmudgeonly sexton?

Our sexton, to begin with, is not quite as unlettered as others see him, or as he would have us believe. He spends his days in and around the beit midrash and in conversation with scholars who devote their time to study. He knows the text of the Hebrew Bible well and can identify the sources of the scriptural quotations that are the rabbi's preferred mode of communication. Difficult verses with original interpretations fall into his mouth ("A verse in the Torah occurred to me") at key moments (35). He fully comprehends all of the rabbi's homilies and textual references, and he is not so humble to observe about himself, "That is one thing I take pride in: if I do not understand our Master's words right away, later on I do" (46). The shamash's religious world has been deeply influenced by the dissemination of Kabbalah into broad sectors of Polish Jewry, and it is natural for him, for example, when he bemoans Aaron's misguided inquiries into the meaning of Jewish suffering, to speak of persecutions as God's way of purging us from the "*qelipot* we have acquired in the lands of the Gentiles and thereby prepare us for the day of His Redemption" (9). Although he repeatedly avers that he is not among the devotees of mystical interpretation (49), he does not hesitate to include the glosses of those who are, and on occasion to offer his own (36). When he looks up at the stars after emerging from the Netherworld, a line occurs to him from the Book of the Angel Razi'el, an early medieval kabbalistic work (see translator's note to p. 36). After he witnesses the tortures of the scholarly sinners in Gehinnom and before the rabbi explains the reason for their fate, the shamash performs a mental search: "I reviewed all the sins and punishments enumerated in the holy books and could find none that matched what I had seen" (32). This is a feat that requires no small amount of learning. His reading is also broad, as demonstrated by his referring to an anecdote in *Sefer kaftor vaferaḥ*, a Hebrew treatise on rabbinic aggadah by Yaakov bar Yitzchak Luzzato, Safed, ca. 1527–1587 (8). In sum, although the shamash is no *talmid ḥakham* in terms of scholarly attainment or class position, he is a creature of the culture of the beit midrash whose literacy enables him to grasp the meaning of all that transpires around him in the beit midrash and its culture. The most eloquent testimony to his literacy is to be found in his reconstruction *from memory* of the memorial ceremonies on the twentieth of Sivan and the many quotations from Scripture and from arcane liturgical poems that attended them.

A source of his power lies, paradoxically, in the meekness of his subservience to Rabbi Moshe. To be sure, the very nature of his office as shamash enjoins this subordination, as does the fact of his youth—he was fifty-four years younger than when he relates the story!—in relation to the rabbi's venerable age when he served him in what turned out to be the last year of the sage's life. Yet the devotion of this proud and irascible man to his master rests on a more compelling foundation. There is a profound affinity of spirit and temperament between master and servant. This is expressed in an area of human interaction that is central to the thematic preoccupation of the story: speech, necessary and unnecessary. Although there are many tasks that the shamash is called on to perform at the rabbi's behest, his intuitive understanding of what is required of him often obviates the need for his instructions to be articulated: "Many times it seemed as though the look in his eyes told what he wanted to say to me" (13). The repertoire of nonverbal communications between the two enables them to use speech only for what is truly worthy to be spoken about: "One did not make small talk with our Master" (13). But it is more than a gift for attunement that enables the shamash to offer such devotion. Rather, it is his identification with the authority the rabbi wields with such utter probity and integrity, and it is in the enforcement of this authority that the shamash finds a calling suited to his temperament. When, as quoted above, the elders of Buczacz express their amazement over the shamash being singled out to witness astonishing sights, the one exception to his ordinariness they note is his temper.

This strikes the reader as an accurate observation. The shamash is indeed a man of intense moral focus who is easily provoked by the temporizing of others. In Rabbi Moshe's rule over Buczacz, he finds a regime with whose righteousness he wholeheartedly identifies, so much so that he can subsume his will within the rabbi's will without feeling diminished. To the contrary, he is nurtured, empowered and elevated by being enlisted in the rabbi's service. After the rabbi gives him the first intimations of their fateful journey, the shamash says to himself, "How good it is to know that we have leaders whose words keep us on the straight path and sustain us in this Exile" (15). Reported a half century later, his words convey to his listeners an implicit critique of current rabbinic regimes and the leadership *they* offer.

The vignette about the melamed and the tax collector in Chapter 4 underscores the affinity between the rabbi's unbowed leadership and the shamash's fierce resolve. The story is told in the context of a conversation between the shamash and his first wife, and it occurs at the moment when the rabbi has told the shamash that he requires his help for a special undertaking, but before there is an inkling of just how special the errand will be. The reason the rabbi gives for enlisting his help is particularly telling: "I know that people do not frighten you" (12). And indeed, when the shamash goes home for breakfast before returning to the rabbi, his nervous preoccupation is noticed by his wife, who engages him in speculating about the mysterious task. In the course of these speculations, she mentions the episode of the melamed and the tax collector, which the shamash now reprises for the reader. The episode concerns a melamed who was slapped in the face by a wealthy man who was disappointed with the results of the melamed's attempts to educate his son. The melamed brought the tax collector to court over the assault, and when the latter failed to show up, "Our Master then instructed me to go and tell the man that if there is no legal accounting here below, there certainly is one up above, and if he would not appear before the local rabbinical court he would absolutely be hauled before the beit din of Gehinnom. So I went to him without the least fear of him or his dogs or his servants" (13). The shamash will shortly discover that the mission for which he is being enlisted will expose him to dangers greater than menacing dogs and nasty servants. Nonetheless, the rabbi has identified within this poor, young and unrecognized assistant an unbowed resoluteness of purpose that can be mobilized for holy purposes.

The shamash's monumental expression of will is the one that the reader might easily take for granted: telling the story that accounts for the great majority of *Hamashal vehanimshal*. This power resides, of course, not merely in the fact of telling the story but rather in the extraordinary capacity to shape and project a narrative that compels his listeners to change their lives. In this he even surpasses his master, the great homilist, whose revered preaching does not approach the shamash's narrative in its electric ability to produce moral self-questioning. Underlying the shamash's astonishing performance is the perplexing question of why he launches into it in the first place. The precipitating events lie in the distant past. Because of the tale's air of dramatic immediacy, we do not realize just how far in the past they lie until the shamash mentions in passing the figure of fifty-four years toward the very end of his narrative. For these many long years, those astounding events had remained secret knowledge guarded by the shamash in accordance with the sacred principles of restraint and discretion in matters of language laid down by Rabbi Moshe.

What impels the shamash to violate those principles and disclose the terrible events of a half century earlier? The story discloses two motives, one explicit and one implicit, and the coexistence of the two explains a great deal about the way the shamash tells his tale. The explicit motive is a moral indignation that pays tribute to the values of the shamash's long-dead master. In the years since the originating events, the shamash has witnessed a drift away from the high principles of restraint in speech that the rabbi had made the thrust of his valedictory address to his flock. Conspicuous displays of learning, as witness by the proliferation of pilpul and ḥidushim, have undercut loyalty to the plain and true meaning of the Torah; the members of the mercantile elite have purchased scholars with these showy talents as husbands for their daughters in order to elevate their family status. That fateful Sabbath morning when one such son-in-law blathers his latest scintillating ḥidush into his friend's ear during the Torah service is simply too much for the shamash. The implicit motive lies in the twin traumas that left their searing impress on him as a youth and a young man: the massacres of 1648 and the journey to Gehinnom. To be sure, as a victim/survivor of 1648, the shamash underwent an ordeal, which is given no back story, that was presumably no worse than that of many other Jews of Buczacz. And that is precisely the important point: Although Buczacz famously escaped the brunt of the physical injury inflicted by Khmelnitski, do not think that the spiritual damage was anything but severe and far-reaching. The shamash is a Buczacz everyman in this regard, and fifty-four years later, when the town is once again teeming and prosperous, he is among the few surviving firsthand witnesses who carry the horrors within them. When it comes to Gehinnom and the gruesome tortures of the ostensibly righteous there, however, the shamash inhabits his own singular category. He has remained silent about these twin traumas for many decades, even as they have presumably never ceased to exert painful pressure on his inner and unconscious life. Although moral indignation provides a respectable trigger for his extraordinary act of public humiliation and the story that follows it, there is much in this outpouring that taps the need for confession and catharsis.

The simultaneous operation of two sets of motivation is critical in explaining a highly problematic hallmark of the shamash's narration: his penchant for digression. Now, having entered the Agnonian universe, the experienced reader may extend wide latitude to this practice, or even simply take it for granted. Yet if we attend to the particular, urgent message of this story, then the question of narrative superfluity becomes marked as moral laxity. After all, the moral the shamash works hard at impressing on his listeners—a moral learned from his master and confirmed by the narrator—is that speech should be husbanded and expended only when necessary. Silence, discretion, reticence, gesture in place of words, Scripture in place of human discourse, the avoidance of speech about others— these are the bywords of a religious seriousness that begins with chatting in the synagogue and exfoliates into an ethics of being in the world. The actual telling of the story itself is the dramatic result of an accidental violation of this principle. The shamash certainly does not intend to tell the story of the journey to Hell that took place a half century earlier; but when his ire is enflamed and he commits an act of public humiliation, he has no recourse but to divulge the events he has kept silent about for so very long. Yet once he is inevitably launched on his narrative of those extraordinary events, the ethics of restraint should, by his own lights, require him to hew closely to his moral message and avoid all extraneous remarks. But the outcome, as any reader can see, is quite otherwise. The shamash's tale is replete with all manner of subsidiary observations, anecdotes and vignettes. Is this simply the old Agnonian charm, the traditional license of the storyteller, beguiling to some and irksome to others?

I would argue that the answer is no in the case of this story, as well as in many others of Agnon's writings. The argument for rationalizing the digressions and viewing them as performing strategic functions rests on the dual nature of the shamash's motivations. His explicit motive is to drive home the moralizing message about the evils of competing with divine speech; his implicit and unconscious motive is to give expression to a variety of traumas and anxieties that include the unexplained reasons for God's having visited so much suffering on His people, the horrific tortures of Gehinnom that are meted out not only to the obviously wicked and the loss of his great mentor and master, together with the decline of true and wise rabbinic authority. These concerns exert pressure on the shamash's intention to tell "the truth and nothing but the truth" and convey what is immediately relevant to the elders of Buczacz; they create a kind of interference in the dissemination of his message. The pattern is evident on almost every page of the story, but nowhere more than in two large narrative blocks. The heartrending story about

Aaron's apostasy is strictly necessary only to explain how the rabbi and shamash came to discover the compartments of Gehinnom that house the scholars who are being punished for hawking their wares during the reading of the Torah. But since Aaron's story is saturated with emotional losses and troubling theological speculations connected to 1648, he cannot desist from giving the account ample room even at the same time he avers that it is not the main point and that he must move on. A similar case is the great block of narrative devoted to depicting the ceremonies of the twentieth of Sivan commemorating the massacres. Loving detail is lavished on all of the difficult piyyutim and on the obscure biblical verses parsed by the rabbi, and in general on the particulars of this epic scene of remembrance. Yet all this bears no relevance to the story's moral teaching about human and divine speech. The two terse parables that do bear on the moral theme seem tacked on at the end of the day's proceedings as if they were afterthoughts. I shall presently explain.

Thus there emerges from the story a differential hermeneutic that enables the reader to make sense of the shamash's digressive habits. What might seem errant and meandering and the sign of a failure of discipline is in fact something else entirely. It is the record of an inner turmoil in which the traumas of the past are continually claiming their due alongside the shamash's efforts to project the more official ethical message. This is a method of reading that provides no small measure of help in negotiating many reaches of the Agnon universe.

MASHAL AS DECOY

In accounting for the meaning of a literary text, we usually take the privileged status of the work's title as axiomatic. We assume that in fashioning a title an author is choosing an evocative phrase that stands for the work as a whole and pointing us in the direction of its main thematic import. In the story before us, Agnon would seem to be playing against those expectations. By titling his story *The Parable and Its Lesson* [*Hamashal vehanimshal*], Agnon invites us to assume that a parabolic homily will serve as the climax of the story's drama or as a central node around which the thematic lines of the story will be arrayed. Yet the title does not do its job, and on completion of the story the reader can be forgiven for feeling duped or at least disoriented. The two parables, the one about an anteater and the other about the lord of a palace, are grotesque and meager, and the abrupt way in which they are delivered after so many events of high moment and drama is the essence of anticlimactic. Can't Agnon do better?

The parable of the anteater is provocative on many levels. As a general principle, the classic rabbinic parable rests on a foundation of familiarity, whether understood in terms of its rhetorical effect or the history of its conventions in homiletic literature. The homilist compares a situation that is simpler and more familiar to his listeners (the *mashal*) to a grave or complex religious message (the *nimshal*). The dynamics of a royal household in which a king banishes his consort or exiles a son who angered him is often compared to the embroiled relations between God and the Jewish people.[24] In Late Antiquity, Jews lived under Roman rule, and although they had little firsthand exposure to the lives of imperial figures, they did understand the absolute authority of the emperor and his regional governors. Over time they became so accustomed to—even fond of—these stereotypical motifs that the parable was looked to as the unit in a long homily that would deliver the most delight.[25] In pointed contrast to this practice, the creature Rabbi Moshe places at the center of his parable is grotesquely unfamiliar several times over. The news of the existence of this creature has been given to him thirdhand by one Reb Zevulun, a spice merchant, who in turn heard about it from caravan operators who ply the desert routes to the Land of Cush. In addition to having its existence rest on hearsay, the creature fits into no known species; it is a variety of monkey that resembles a dog and survives by eating ants. Jarring as well is the violence with which the creature lures its unsuspecting, industrious little victims into its trap and then suddenly foments their deaths. The rabbi's laconic and hurried presentation of the nimshal, the allegorical solution to the parable, is also strange. There is no reference made to the problem the rabbi announced he was setting out to address—the sin of improper speech—and the dramatic emphasis in the nimshal falls entirely on the tragic inevitability of antlike Jews falling into the infernal trap laid for them.

Then, having missed the mark with his first parable, the rabbi marshals his energies and offers a second parable, which, this time around, succeeds on every level. The parable tells the story of the lord of a castle who takes pity on a poor man and listens to his tale of woes; the lord not only allows him to settle on his estate but provides him with writs that grant him hereditary ownership of his property. But the poor man ends by alienating the lord's good will when he talks about irrelevant matters and then interrupts the lord as the lord reads from the documents that assure the poor man's future fortune. For his listeners this time, the figures in the parable are reassuringly familiar and transparent. The theme of the parable is decidedly "on message." And the rabbi skillfully exploits the resources of the mashal-nimshal structure so as to produce a gasp of recognition when his listeners, having recognized the evident foolishness of the poor man's conduct, realize that they are he, and that by jabbering in the synagogue they endanger their hold on the gifts God has bestowed on them.

Rabbi Moshe has finally hit the mark. But why did he fail to get it right the first time? The answer becomes evident if we stand back and view the anteater parable in the larger context of the lengthy commemorative ceremonies on the twentieth of Sivan. The parables come at the very end, at a point where the rabbi has announced that he is shifting from the theme of mourning and memorialization to the theme of synagogue worship and its disturbances. The import of the first parable clearly indicates, starkly and dolefully, that despite his intentions the rabbi has not succeeded in making the shift. His deepest thoughts remain entangled in and possessed by the horrible losses of 1648 and the troubling theological questions they raise, questions that have already led to the apostasy and death of his favorite student. How could those gentle and industrious ants, so admired by King Solomon in his proverbs, have known that the sand hill they swarmed upon was in fact a satanic trap? "And yet with all their wisdom, the ants cannot avoid falling into the hands of the monkey" (53). The source of their livelihood suddenly becomes their grave when the creature rouses itself from its camouflaged hiding place and shuts the trap. In its evocation of gruesome violence and disorienting astonishment, the parable is supremely effective, but only if we think of it as serving the sermonic agenda the rabbi has announced he was moving *beyond*.

Again we are confronted with the memories of 1648 welling up unbidden and interfering with the moral message the story seeks to broadcast. The shared wish of the narrator, the shamash and the rabbi to hew to the moral message is a desire they can only imperfectly fulfill. They seek to do so nevertheless because of the portentous theological issues at stake. Rabbi Moshe can skillfully offer the standard consolations about repentance and God's abiding love for Israel, but he is powerless to mitigate the terrible losses and the terrible memories, and when it comes to sensitive and inquisitive souls such as Aaron, he cannot avert the corrosive spread of theological doubt with its calamitous consequences. This sense of wayward ungovernability is precisely what is absent from the call to refrain from mixing human speech with divine speech in the synagogue. The latter is a question of comportment and discipline; it may pose a challenge to the grandiosity of some scholars, but it is inscribed wholly within the realm of human choice. The mechanisms of moral introspection and fulfillment of religious duty operate on a psychological level very different from traumatic loss and memory. True, the duty to avoid improper speech is not without its frightening aspects. The horrific punishments for transgression, as the shamash has so powerfully witnessed, can seem inexplicably disproportionate to the offense, and the offense itself may be inevitably wired into human behavior. Nevertheless, of the two contending themes of the story, moral challenge is the more optimistic and less demoralizing because it admits of the possibility of corrective human action. When it comes to what God allowed to be done to the Jews in 1648, however, there could be no nostrums.

Why in fact, at the end of this very long fast, does the rabbi introduce a subject that has no ostensible connection to the theme of the day? If he seeks to turn away from imponderable matters of historical suffering and toward governable matters of practical religious conduct, there are undoubtedly any number of areas of spiritual laxity that need shoring up. It is far from clear that in the community of Buczacz at that moment the temptation to speak during the reading of the Torah has the status of a clear and present danger. For when the rabbi begins to turn his attention to the subject he goes so far as to admit that, even though he has heard of the problem, he himself has not seen it with his own eyes (47). The rabbi, to be sure, is in possession of secret knowledge that the townspeople are not privy to. In his journey to Gehinnom, he has seen graphic evidence of the severity of the issue and its persistence over many centuries. It is this long view that may account for why the rabbi, whose last public discourse this is before his death six months later, insists on addressing an area of conduct that is not an acute need of the present moment. Now, Rabbi Moshe is a holy sage who, at least in the shamash's mind, is endowed with *ruaḥ haqodesh*, prophetic foresight. Is it not then possible that the rabbi is in fact directing his words not to the present faithful of Buczacz, the meager remnants of the massacres, the community of two hundred souls who stand as they listen to rabbi's long homily because their synagogue does not yet have chairs or benches, but rather to the Buczacz of some fifty-four years later, whose inhabitants have multiplied and whose merchants have grown prosperous enough to forget when the word of God takes precedence over the casuistry of their sons-in-law?

This speculation gives birth to another speculation. The depiction of the rabbi comes to us wholly through the eyes and lips of the shamash, who selects behaviors, incidents and quotations in order to construct the figure of his venerated master. The shamash lives long into the period of Buczacz's reconstruction and prosperity even as he observes disturbing signs of spiritual complacency in matters concerning which he knows there are dire consequences. Might not the shamash have exercised a preemptive prophetic wisdom on behalf of the rabbi? Might not the parables that concluded the rabbi's long discourse have been "retrofitted" through the work of the imagination to yield an older wisdom that would have the *éclat* of prophetic authority when they would be most needed?

Whatever their etiology, the parables can in no meaningful sense be construed to constitute the climax of the story, or the distillation of its meaning, or the banner under which the reader first encounters the text. As a title, *The Parable and Its Lesson* [*Hamashal vehanimshal*] is a decoy or a counter that draws our attention away from the unstable and contending binaries of the story.

THE HOLY COMMUNITY OF BUCZACZ

As the shamash concludes his tale and the narrator resumes direct narration of the story, a new character moves to center stage: the holy community of Buczacz. One of the great questions that haunts Agnon's epic cycle of Buczacz stories as a whole is whether a community can in fact be conceived of as a character and function like one. Can a social organism exercise the will and agency that we associate with the great figures of fiction? Can a town meaningfully function as the protagonist of a formidable cycle of stories? *'Ir umelo'ah* is the large canvas on which Agnon experiments with this proposition. Although we can reckon with these questions only by taking the whole cycle into account, the final sections of our story give us a glimpse how this collective portraiture might work.

The last four chapters of the story (24–27) present a complex picture of how the community of Buczacz absorbs and processes the extraordinary new information revealed by the shamash's tale. Throughout these pages, Buczacz is spoken about as a single collective, as when the narrator begins Chapter 24 with the statement "The shamash's words left Buczacz astounded" (*'amdah Bitshatsh temihah*, 58); or when verbs in the third person plural are used to convey concerted action on the part of the inhabitants of the town as a whole. Although the distinct behavior of some subgroups is pointed out, the corporate identity of Buczacz is maintained throughout.

The first response of Buczacz is cognitive disorientation. It was always taken for granted that "talking generally brings people together and dispels worry, while silence is usually a sign of sorrow and suffering" (58–59), and now this commonsense conviction has been powerfully refuted. Dealing with the contradiction brings out the dialectical acumen of the town, and it is in the course of their arguments that they come to admit the logic of the shamash's arguments and acknowledge how even learned human discourse can become an affront to God's honor and generosity. After having grasped the point intellectually, they begin to confront the dread and anxiety that inevitably follow in the wake of this realization.

> A series of groans came forth from the assembled. First from despair, and then from trepidation, for even when one takes care not to talk during the services or the Torah reading, there are times when one simply cannot control oneself and things that serve purposes neither lofty nor base come out. (59)

Reviewing their Sabbath morning practices with an honest eye, the townspeople are constrained to admit that rarely a week goes by when some words of the Torah reading are not drowned out or otherwise lost by well-meaning (or sarcastic) remarks correcting the reader and by the commotion they provoke.

Within this general spiritual reckoning, there are those who are especially receptive to this heightened stringency because they have already intuited its truth but not yet grasped its enormity. They not only immediately take upon themselves the rule of silence in synagogue but, in a way that would have gratified the shamash's master Rabbi Moshe, also extend the principle of avoiding unnecessary speech to behavior in the marketplace and in the home. At the same time, there are others in the community who, while accepting the validity of the new stricture, give themselves over to an obsessive and even lurid fascination with the details of Gehinnom. Are there fallen angels there? Are the tortures interrupted on the Sabbath? Do they say the same prayers we do? What happens to their clothes and their fringed undergarments after their bodies cease to exist? "There was no end to their questions," the narrator informs us, "and because they had not yet learned to restrain their tongues, those

tongues nattered on with abandon" (61). Absorbed in the sensational revelations of the shamash's tale, they have allowed the real import of the
story to pass by them.

Yet, in the final analysis, the townspeople of Buczacz do the right
thing. They recognize that the shamash's precipitating act of public humiliation was in fact a gesture of self-sacrifice, and instead of fining him
and removing him from his office, they restore him to public honor and
give him the special task of standing on the bimah during the Torah
reading and vigilantly surveying the congregation for errant instances of
idle chatter. This is but one instance of the procedures and safeguards the
elders put into effect so that the new discipline will be made a permanent
part of the religious life of the town.

The willingness of Buczacz to rectify its ways, in other words, gives
the story a happy ending, at least in the classic sense in which the bonds
of society are reconstituted after a threat to their cohesion. It remains
unclear, however, whether the positive ending outweighs the grave instances of suffering so strongly adduced earlier in the story concerning
the aftermath of 1648 and in the compartments of Gehinnom. These
two sources of tragic undertow, we have seen, contend at every level
of the story with the moral issue of divine and human speech, the former the result of ungovernable forces and the latter more susceptible to
human agency. Through his narrator, Agnon formerly converts the story
into a comedy by devoting the final chapters to the successful repentance
of the town. In metaphysical and aesthetic terms, however, the ending comes across as less of a consummation than an act of will. To the
threat posed by the corrosive and deconstructive forces of unexplained
suffering—in this world and the next—the story offers the example of
Buczacz as a *qehilah qedoshah*, a holy community that is imperfect but
capable of religious renewal.

In the privileging of religious rationality in the concluding chapters
of the story, some readers may find a disappointing falloff in aesthetic
interest. For after the melodrama of a court trial and a descent into Hell,
the efforts to reform synagogue protocols may seem lacking in dramatic

moment, or smacking of a tacked-on happy ending. Yet this ending, on closer inspection, turns out to be less than wholly consummate and accomplished. Although the community makes amends and institutes many reforms, the spirit of those corrections are eclipsed over time by the realities of communal life. Synagogues cannot subsist without contributions from congregants, and these are generally made when a man is called to the Torah and given the opportunity to have blessings publicly recited for the well-being of the members of his household. In a sardonically funny passage (64), the narrator catalogues the many ways in which this seemingly benign practice can result in propagating waves of distraction and animosity. This report on the equivocal fate of the reforms over time not only reconfirms the narrator's reliability as a jaundiced observer but also leavens the story's positive resolution by grounding it in the realities of human nature and communal behavior.

The apotheosis of the shamash and the restoration of his office and honor camouflage a similar uncertainty. Beset by endless questions about the afterlife, most of them maddeningly trivial, the shamash has to decide how much of what he discovered about Gehinnom he is willing to give up to these inquisitive and intrusive townspeople. Although he would much prefer to abide by the ethos of discretion and restraint, he knows that without disclosing secrets he has no chance of stoking the will to repent. He has, after all and for ostensibly higher ends, broken his decades-long silence and told the shocking tale of the descent into the Netherworld. The last glimpse the narrator gives us of the shamash finds him meditating on the mysteries of divine indirection that have brought him and his tale to the center of attention, and this even though he was merely a candle holder to the rabbi in his audacious mission to release an agunah from her bonds.

The shamash is well aware that it is the sensational revelations about the afterlife that have been the engine for the town's new moral resolve. The townspeople of Buczacz have been riveted by his story because all human beings are fascinated by suffering, sin and punishment, the stranger and more grotesque the better. There is no denying that it is the perverse pleasure people derive from such tales that makes them willing to attend to the moral message. But that kind of pleasure is only a provocative stimulant; it does not provide the inner resources for sustained change. "Such pleasure has been the downfall of many," the shamash observes and then goes on to posit, "But there are many kinds of pleasure, and happy is the one whose pleasure brings him edification and whose edification is his pleasure" (62). In the shamash's wistful sigh, we can hear the prayerful wish of many writers who would hope their readers derive as much aesthetic gratification from the nuanced description of the everyday lives of their characters seeking to reform their lives as from the melodramatic events that precipitated the desire to change. This sentiment would not be out of place, for example, in the mouth of George Eliot's narrator in *Middlemarch* as she describes the long night of Dorothea Brooke's moral reckoning with herself and its prosaic aftermath. It is the particular burden Agnon takes on himself in *'Ir umelo'ah* as he seeks to make the life of a holy community interesting and important to us, even if in the process he supplies us with no small stock of the shocking and the deviant.

INSCRIPTION, CATASTROPHE, RETELLING

On the last page of *Hamashal vehanimshal* we discover that the story we have been reading is the work of a writer living in modern-day Jerusalem, a city filled with its own share of noisy synagogues. This is a disorienting discovery. Although we "know" that we have been reading a text by S. Y. Agnon, a twentieth-century Hebrew writer, the story all along has been told by a narrator close to the events in the seventeenth century, who, in turn, hands over most of the narration to an eyewitness; it is a world in which we have been fully immersed. What is the relationship between the narrator, in whose grip we have been held throughout this remarkable tale, and the writer, who pokes his head up at the very conclusion? Is the former merely a creation or a device of the latter? Our disorientation is compounded when we are informed that the story we have read is not the original story but rather a replacement for the original story that was inscribed in the pinqas of Buczacz and lost in the Holocaust. What is the relationship between the original and its replacement?

Most of what we know about the lost text revolves around the office of the scribe and his role in formulating the account of the shamash's story that is inscribed in the communal register. The narrator is unstinting in his praise for the scribe's work. "So the scribe wrote out the whole story in words true and wise, in the way words were used in Buczacz at the time when Buczacz was Buczacz. Some of the words were from the Torah, some from the sages, all of them had an eloquence that gives tongue to knowledge" (66). The scribe takes the events of the shamash's tale as his raw material and submits them to a process of sublimation whereby they are recast into a more exalted style that draws directly from the language of sacred texts. The calligraphy itself is the result of the scribe's unrelenting drive to perfection, with "each letter distinct unto itself and each one in its place on the line, like people standing for the silent devotion." The elders of Buczacz proceed to show the scribe's handiwork to the wise men of the day throughout Poland, who pronounce its style and grammar above reproach.

We can only imagine what that text was like, yet, having read the story before us, we can have a strong presumption about what it does *not* contain. In the effort to fashion an exemplary tale that foregrounds its religious message, the lost text likely eliminated most of the elements that makes the story fascinating to us as modern readers: the digressions and obiter dicta of the shamash's narrative through which the personal and collective anxieties of the times find their unofficial expression. Eliminated too would have been many (unsolved!) mysteries large and small: How could Zlateh's *get* (ritual divorce) have been given by Aaron if his death was confirmed by the visit to Gehinnom? How do the rabbi and shamash emerge from Gehinnom unscathed? Why does the shamash wait fifty-four years to tell his story? How did he come to marry Zlateh? Now, with all due respect to the perfection of the scribe's text and with all due respect to the destruction of the holy community of Buczacz, few of us would wish to have that text restored if it meant giving up the story we have just read. As the shamash himself wisely said, there is pleasure and there is pleasure. To subsist on the pleasure of edification alone, even combined with exquisite calligraphy, is an option many of us would forgo.

Nonetheless, our knowledge of Buczacz, our understanding of the time when "Buczacz was Buczacz," is not diminished by our having acquired it through our reading a story written by a modern author. To make the ironic point sharper, it is *only* through this modern act of imaginative writing that we can make a connection to the world of Buczacz. It is through the fountain pen that coyly beckons to the author on the story's last page that the town comes alive, rather than through the quill and ink pot of the scribe. But if the means of inscription are different, Agnon gamely insists on an essential continuity, if not identity, between these two offices, both of which are represented by the word *sofer*. When the Hebrew language was modernized in the nineteenth century and an equivalent was sought for the new vocation of "writer," it was decided to stick with *sofer* rather than invent a new term. It would be left to context alone to determine if a particular use of the word indicated the God-fearing artisan who meticulously calligraphed Torah scrolls, tefillin and mezuzot or whether it indicated the modern author of novels, short stories and feuilletons. For Agnon, the confusion fitted perfectly.

1648 AND THE HOLOCAUST

By leaving mention of the Holocaust to the last page of his story, Agnon exercised a canny circumspection. He did not want the trauma of 1648 to be backlit by the later catastrophe, or reduced to being a foreshadowing. This of course does not prevent us (belated readers of the story, saturated with Holocaust consciousness) from doing so. But the experience of reading the story should, I think, urge upon us restraint. If anything, Agnon wants us to work the relationship between the two events in reverse. We should take the horrific knowledge imprinted on us from the events of the twentieth century and use it in the service of understanding a calamity in the distant and unfamiliar seventeenth century.

> I pondered the possibility that the Gehinnom of our time would make
> us forget the Gehinnom that the shamash saw, and the story about it,
> and all we can learn from that story. (68)

There is something uncanny as well about the span of time between
the two events and the acts of memory that follow them. Between 1648
and the Holocaust is an arc of almost exactly three hundred years. The descent into Gehinnom takes place in the immediate aftermath of the massacres—let us say ten years later—and the shamash's telling of the story
fifty-four years later. Agnon wrote *The Parable and Its Lesson* in the mid-
1950s—it was serialized in *Haaretz* in 1958—and here we are reading and
interpreting it a half century or so later. What is this correspondence
meant to tell us? To begin with, it sets up a correspondence between Buczacz in the aftermath of 1648 and Israel, where Agnon is writing the story
in the aftermath of the murder of European Jewry. In Buczacz, although
the memory of the horrific recent events permeates Jewish life, the community is struggling successfully to reconstitute itself and rehabilitate the
institutions of Jewish worship and study. In Israel, although the struggle
to make the young state into a secure refuge for the Jewish people is bearing fruit, remembrance of the Holocaust has been pushed to the margins, as has religious culture and practice as well. In this complex analogy,
which can be developed in a number of directions, Buczacz emerges as a
precursor to Israel, vulnerable to Gentile violence, yes, but autonomous
and living under the sway of Torah.[26] Israel, in turn, becomes the succes-
sor to Buczacz whose mission it is to perpetuate the full and autonomous
living of Jewish life without dependence on the gentiles. This is a dialectic
that moves forward and backward in time and transcends the received
dichotomy between a decaying and moribund diaspora and a Jewish state
born of revolutionary Zionism.

A reading of *The Parable and Its Lesson* in the context of the larger
project of *A City in Its Fullness* shows us the difference between Holocaust
literature and Jewish literature provoked by the Holocaust. By their very
nature, Holocaust fiction, memoir and testimony, whether in words or
video images, focus on the war years and their aftermath. Only in some

cases is memory pushed back to the generation of the parents or the grandparents, and then often in the service of shaping a family idyll that is subsequently shattered. For Agnon, the spiritual power of European Jewry, now after its utter eradication, lay farther back in time, much farther than human remembrance can reach. We must therefore rely on the literary imagination and the protean powers of the story, as told in Hebrew, the historical language of the Jewish people, to enter the world that was lost.

NOTES

1. Gershon Shaked, *Shmuel Yosef Agnon: A Revolutionary Traditionalist* (New York: New York University Press, 1989).

2. Jerusalem: Schocken, 1973. The title is a phrase from the Hebrew Bible, but where it comes from is less simple than meets the eye. The only location where the exact phrase is found is in a stinging prophecy of condemnation against the Northern Kingdom in Amos (6:8): "My Lord swears by Himself: I loathe the Pride of Jacob, and I detest its fortresses. I will declare forfeit city and inhabitants alike ['*ir umelo'ah*]" (JPS). The word *umelo'ah* itself is most familiar from the declarative opening line of Psalm 24, the coronation hymn sung in the synagogue when returning the Torah to the ark on holidays. There *umelo'ah* occurs in a bound phrase with *erets*: "The earth is the Lord's and the fullness thereof" (King James). That bound phrase *erets umelo'ah* occurs another eight times in Scripture. Since Agnon's evident purpose in this book is to elevate and sanctify the name of his town, he can hardly mean us to think about the corrupt and condemned city of Amos' prophecy. By a barely perceptible sleight of hand, Agnon has taken the familiar ecstatic pronouncement about the earth and the fullness thereof and substituted city for earth; all the while we assume—both correctly and mistakenly—that he has simply plucked and transcribed a piece of Scripture. The point of the maneuver is to emphasize that it is a city, *his* city, that he has come to extol. Whereas the psalm famously declares that the earth and its fullness are the Lord's, whether the same goes for the city that has been substituted for the earth is not as clear.

3. Quoted in Edward Said, *On Late Style: Music and Literature Against the Grain* (New York: Vintage, 2006), p. 8.

4. Arnold Band, *Nostalgia and Nightmare: A Study in the Fiction of S. Y. Agnon* (Berkeley and Los Angeles: University of California Press, 1968), pp. 330–366.

5. Among the most important of these are *Beḥanuto shel mar Lublin*, *'Ad henah*, *Kisui hadam*, *'Ad 'olam*, *Eido veEinam*, and *Hadom vekhise*.

6. A select list of critical reactions to the book when it appeared includes Yehudah Friedlander, "Masekhet shivah ufreidah" [Return and Leave Taking], *Ha'aretz*, June 1, 1973; and "A City and the Fullness Thereof," *Hebrew Book Review* (Tel Aviv), Autumn 1973, pp. 3–6; Hillel Barzel, "'*Ir umelo'ah*: 'uvdah uvedayah" [Ir umeloah: Fact and Invention], *Yediyot Aḥaronot*, September 26, 1973; Yaakov Rabi, "Hatorah, ha'emunah, vemirmat hatsedaqah" [Torah, Belief, and the Dishonesty of Charity], *'Al Hamishmar*, October 12, 1973; Yisrael Cohen, "Haḥavayah ha'arkhtipit shel '*Ir umelo'ah*" [The Archetypal World of '*Ir umelo'ah*], *Moznayim*, Vol. 28, Nos. 1–2 (Dec.–Jan. 1973–74), pp. 61–73; A. Y. Brawer, "'*Ir umelo'ah*: 'olam shene'elam" ['*Ir umelo'ah*: A World That Disappeared], *Ha'umah*, April 1974, pp. 246–253.

7. Dan Laor, *Ḥayyei 'Agnon* [A Life of Agnon] (Jerusalem and Tel Aviv: Schocken, 1998), p. 408.

8. The story began as a fragment, also called "Hasiman," which appeared in *Moznayim* (Iyyar/Sivan [May] 1944), p. 104. The full story, with its forty-two sections, appeared in S. Y. Agnon, *Ha'eish veha'eitsim* (Jerusalem and Tel Aviv: Schocken, 1962), pp. 283–312. Translated by Arthur Green in Alan Mintz and Anne Golomb Hoffman (eds.), S. Y. Agnon: *A Book That Was Lost: Thirty-Five Stories* (New Milford, CT: Toby Press, 2008), pp. 397–429.

9. I have argued this point in my *Ḥurban: Responses to Catastrophe in Hebrew Literature* (Syracuse: Syracuse University Press, 1996).

10. For an expansion of this theses, see chapter 2 ("Two Models in the Study of Holocaust Representation") in my *Popular Culture and the Shaping of Holocaust Memory in America* (Seattle: University of Washington Press, 2001).

11. *Abyss of Despair* (*Yeven metsulah*), trans. Abraham J. Mesch (New York: Bloch, 1950).

12. The narrator as a chronicler allied with the communal register was already employed to great advantage in Hebrew literature by Micha Yosef Berdichevsky. See the story "Parah adumah" in *Kitvei Mikhah Yosef Bin-Gurion (Berdichevsky)* (Tel Aviv: Dvir, 1975), pp. 181–184.

13. The story originally appeared in *Haaretz* on September 14, October 5, and December 5, 1958.

14. Literally in the Hebrew: the meat was still between his teeth and undigested. The reference is to Numbers 11:33, which describes the unrestrained cravings of the

Israelites for meat. A more contemporary example would be Abraham Joshua Heschel's celebration of East European Jewish piety in his *The Earth Is the Lord's* (New York: H. Schuman, 1950).

15. The pedagogical passion for fashioning a mode of communication that is precisely fitted to his listeners is made the subject of an anecdote, a mashal of sorts, about a Jewish jeweler who is summoned to create gold earrings for the king's daughter and takes special pains to adapt the ornament to the exact proportions of her ear (414).

16. Shulamit Almog argues that Rabbi Moshe does not make practical use of his eyewitness knowledge of Aaron's death because he realizes that matters of Jewish law must be adjudicated according to evidence and procedures that are transparent and available to all. Despite the rabbi's intense empathy for Zlateh, he knows that supernatural disclosures that he alone—together with the shamash—have been privy to cannot meet this standard of evidence. See Shulamit Almog, *'Ir, mishpat, sipur* [City, Law, Story] (Tel Aviv: Schocken, 2002), pp. 78–82.

17. Joshua Shanes, "Buchach," YIVO Encyclopedia of Eastern Europe, http://www.yivoencyclopedia.org/article.aspx/Buchach; Martin Rudner, "Buczacz Origins," http://www.ibiblio.org/yiddish/Places/Buczacz/bucz-p1.htm.

18. Literally, the persecutions of 5408 and 5409.

19. Shanes, ibid.

20. This is a rich theme in Agnon's corpus. At the conclusion of *Oreah natah lalun* [A Guest for the Night] the keys to the study house of Buczacz, which has been decimated by World War One, are transferred to Eretz Yisrael. In the opening, foundational story of *'Ir umelo'ah* ("Buczacz," pp.9–13), the founding of the city is framed as a way station on an ascent to Eretz Yisrael that became permanent.

21. For a responsible overview of these issues with representative texts, see Simcha Paull Raphael, *Jewish Views of the Afterlife* (Northvale, NJ: Jason Aronson, 1994), especially chapter 6, "Visionary Tours of the Afterlife in Medieval Midrash," pp. 163–232.

22. *Qetsat qasheh,* "a little difficult," is a phrase that has its origins in the Tosafists' commentary on the Talmud; it is used when the Tosafists find glaring contradictions or problems in Rashi's commentary. It is a classic instance of understatement. Within a religious tradition based on the presumed authority of earlier teachers, the phrase is a delicate means of noting a major issue. See "Hasiman" [The Sign], 714, for an interesting parallel.

23. The other outstanding example of the overall narrator handing over the narration to a narrator dramatized within the story is "Ha'ish levush habadim" [The Linen Man, 84–121].

24. David Stern, *Parables in Midrash: Narrative and Exegesis in Rabbinic Literature* (Cambridge, MA: Harvard University Press, 1991).

25. This is wonderfully dramatized in the story "Genizah" by Devorah Baron, *Parshiyot: sipurim mequbatsim* [Collected Stories] (Jerusalem: Bialik Institute, 1951), pp. 236–245. Also note to pp.424–425, where the shamash digresses on the rabbi's championing the mashal as a homiletic tool superior to the rhetoric of reproach (tokhehah). It is worth noting that the narrator intervenes immediately after this remark to point out that midrash collections were scarce in the rabbi's time, whereas today all recognize the worth of the mashal. In the story "Hamevakshim lahem rav" in *'Ir umelo'ah*, a letter of rabbinic appointment specifies the obligation to include aggadah and meshalim in public homilies in anticipation of an inclination of scholarly rabbis to speak only of matters of halakhah.

26. In the very first story in *'Ir umelo'ah*, "Buczacz," the founding of the city is presented as resulting from an arrested pilgrimage to the Land of Israel.

GLOSSARY

Agunah Literally a "chained woman"; a woman who cannot remarry because her husband will not grant her a divorce, or because the fact of his death has not been conclusively established.

Alfasi Isaac Alfasi, eleventh-century talmudist active in Fez, Morocco.

Ashkenaz The Jewish communities along the Rhine Valley in the tenth to thirteenth centuries that were formidable centers of Talmud study.

Av Beit Din The head of a rabbinic court, usually the presiding rabbi of a community.

Avodah Worship.

Beit din Rabbinic court.

Beit midrash Study house.

Bimah A raised platform in the synagogue where the Torah is read.

Dayan Judge in a Jewish court.

Etrog A citrus fruit essential to the observance of the Sukkot festival; it is similar but not identical to a lemon.

Gabbai A volunteer official who oversees the finances of a synagogue and directs the allocation of honors.

Gan Eden Paradise (lit. the Garden of Eden).

Gehinnom The Netherworld, Hell.

Haftarah A portion from the Prophets read after the weekly reading from the Pentateuch on Sabbath mornings.

Halakhah Jewish law and jurisprudence.

Havdalah A ceremony, recited Saturday after sundown, using a candle, spices and wine, that separates the Sabbath from the weekdays.

Hidush An interpretation that presents a new insight on a classic text.

Hoshana Rabba The seventh day of the autumn festival of Sukkot.

Kaddish Prayer of praise in Aramaic; also recited by mourners.

Kohen (pl. kohanim) A descendant of the priests who served in the Jerusalem Temple.

Ma'asim tovim Good deeds. Maskilim (sing. maskil) The literate elite in the Jewish community.

Melamed A teacher of young children.

Mezuzah Small box containing a parchment scroll attached to doorways.

Midrash The exegetical and storytelling component of rabbinic texts.

Mikvah Ritual bath used monthly by women after their menses.

Mishnah The code of Jewish law compiled in Palestine around 200 CE. The text for which the Talmud serves as a commentary.

Mitzvot Commanded deeds; generally, the daily acts a Jew is obliged to perform under Jewish law.

Pilpul Clever dialectical solutions to textual problems, often verging on sophistry.

Rashi Acronym of Rabbi Shlomo Yitzhaki, the famous eleventh-century French commentator on the Bible and the Talmud.

Shamash Sexton of a synagogue and assistant to a rabbi.

Shavuot Festival seven weeks following Passover marking the giving of the Torah at Sinai.

Sukkah Booths in which meals are eaten during the festival of Sukkot.

Sukkot The harvest festival that takes place the week following Yom Kippur.

Talit (pl. talitot) Shawl with four fringes worn by men during morning prayer.

Targum An Aramaic translation of the Bible that is traditionally studied along with the Hebrew when studying the weekly portion of the Torah.

Tefillin Black leather boxes and straps containing biblical verses written on parchment, worn by men on the arm and the head during morning prayers.

Tsadik (pl. tsadikim) A righteous person who excels in his relationships both to God and to man.

Yahrzeit The anniversary of the death of a family member.

Yeshivah (pl. yeshivot) Academies of advanced Talmud study.

Yizkor Memorial prayer for the dead recited on major festivals.

Zohar The central text of medieval Jewish mysticism.